1914-1918

WORLD WAR I
told with pictures
by Irving Werstein

COOPER SQUARE PUBLISHERS, INC.

NEW YORK · 1966

DISTRIBUTED BY POCKET BOOKS, INC.

This book is for
CANDIDA DONADIO
Friend, Advisor and Agent

Second Edition
Copyright © 1964 by Cooper Square Publishers, Inc.
59 Fourth Avenue, New York 3, N. Y.
Book designed by Normand F. Lareau
Jacket by H. Lawrence Hoffman
Library of Congress Catalogue Card No. 63-22595
Printed in the United States of America

BEFORE THE STORM 1871-1914

"We are living in a remarkable time," a Swiss journalist wrote in February, 1914. "Not since 1871—except for the Balkans, where war is a way of life—has there been a conflict in Europe; and not since the time of Napoleon, a century ago, have we had a general war."

Such an era of peace was indeed remarkable for Europe, where the major powers, France, Germany, Russia and Austria-Hungary had huge conscript armies and generals who spent days, weeks, even months, working out plans to attack one or the other.

Aloof, yet watchful, was Great Britain. The British had no conscript army; her small regular force was scattered across the expanse of the empire upon which the sun never set. As always, Britain depended upon her navy, the greatest in the world, to safeguard her interests, no matter where.

The absence of war in Europe did not mean tranquility. Although there had been no important hostilities, peace was only a veneer; beneath the surface a volcano rumbled.

In the four decades since the Franco-Prussian War, the age-old hatred of France toward Germany had not abated in the least. The French vowed revenge for the humiliation of 1871 when the Prussian Chancellor, Prince Otto von Bismarck, who had created a united Germany out of a dozen independent dukedoms

The French surrender at Sedan in 1870 during the Franco-Prussian War marked the downfall of Emperor Louis Napoleon III, the establishment of the French Republic and the rise of Germany masterminded by Prince Otto von Bismarck, seated at the head of the table, facing the defeated French generals.

and kingdoms, crushed France in the brief Franco-Prussian War.

Bismarck, the man of "Blood and Iron," exacted a harsh peace from France; the ore- and coal-rich mining provinces of Alsace-Lorraine were taken from France and huge sums of money paid out in reparations.

The Franco-Prussian War toppled the French emperor, Louis Napoleon, from his throne and made that nation a Republic. Bismarck's stern treatment of France assured Germany's position as the most powerful and influential country on the Continent; but it also sparked within the heart of every Frenchman a spirit of revenge against the *boches*—the Germans.

The general who had led the victorious Prussian army in 1870, Graf Helmuth von Moltke, declared, "What our sword has won in half a year, our sword must guard for half a century—and perhaps even longer."

Bismarck headed off the French by forging the Triple Alliance of Germany, Austria-Hungary and Italy. Against this power bloc, France came to an understanding with Russia—forming the so-called Dual Alliance; at the same time, Great Britain and France created the *Entente Cordiale*; this grew into the *Triple Entente* of France, England and Russia. England could no longer stand aside, splendidly isolated; for in 1890, two years after he became emperor of Germany, Kaiser Wilhelm II dismissed Bismarck and took the nation's destinies into his own hands.

Kaiser Wilhelm had great ambitions for Germany. He wanted a colonial empire to match Great Britain's; his dream envisioned as German, all Middle Africa, including the Belgian Congo and Rhodesia; he saw a Berlin-to-Bagdad railway giving Germany access to the oil fields of the Mid-East and complete domination in the Balkans.

The Kaiser cast eyes on the wheatfields of Poland

This painting by A. de Neuville depicts an incident of the Franco-Prussian War in which outnumbered French soldiers make a futile defense of their position against the oncoming Germans seen at the right.

Kaiser Wilhelm II, of the Hohenzollern dynasty, became Emperor of Germany in 1888 at the age of 29. He followed in the steps of his grandfather, Wilhelm I, and father, Freidrich III, both of whom died that same year. Wilhelm II frequently stated his belief that "the sword was mightier than the pen."

Czar Nicholas of Russia and his cousin, George V of England, posed for this picture several years before the outbreak of the First World War, never suspecting that one day they would be allied in the bloodiest conflict ever fought.

and the Ukraine. He meant to make the Baltic states into German dependencies. In the West, the coal mining and industrial areas of northeastern France and Belgium offered tempting targets for expansion.

Bismarck had sought the same objectives with one major difference: he moved diplomatically and destroyed his victims one at a time. Bismarck was a master of deception, he made few enemies. The Kaiser managed to make enemies on every side; he was a broadaxe and Bismarck, a rapier.

The Germans made no secret of their intentions, for Kaiser Wilhelm was a boastful and arrogant man. He launched a naval construction program "to make Germany the master of the seas" and built an army that was the most powerful military machine in the history of the world. German industry was geared to supply it with the best and most modern weapons.

The giant Krupp Works turned out monstrously sized cannon and the Skoda Plant in Austria-Hungary, Germany's chief ally, made guns unmatched in the long history of warfare.

The German General Staff under General Graf Alfred von Schlieffen had drawn up plans for conquest, minutely detailed with a timetable of movement that was a monument to Germanic efficiency.

The Kiel Canal, through which the German navy

had access to the North Sea, was widened to allow the passage of the largest dreadnoughts (battleships). If no other power on the continent was totally prepared for war, the Germans were ready by 1910. The Kaiser only needed a good reason to start a conflict.

He was to wait until 1914 when a random spark set off the powder keg. Before that explosion subsided, dynasties were to fall; millions would be dead and crippled, homeless and uprooted; and the seeds of a second, even greater cataclysm, sown. Within a single generation another world war touched off by Germany would again ravage the tortured earth.

Incredibly, although many men foresaw the catastrophe of 1914-1918, none tried to forestall it. In the forty years of restive European peace, nations seemed more concerned with keeping a precarious balance of power based on guns, bayonets, armies and navies, than to find a means of preventing the holocaust.

All Europe—and the world—was riding on a toboggan of doom; and no man reached for the brake. The Kaiser plotted, the French conspired, the Russians intrigued and the British schemed. In January, 1914 an American observer, after visiting the capitals of Europe, prophetically wrote ". . . we are standing on the brink of disaster . . . the storm is gathering . . . any moment, the full fury of it will strike. . . ."

THE FATAL DAY

Death came to Archduke Franz Ferdinand, and his wife the Duchess Sophie of Hohenberg, on the bright Sunday afternoon of June 28, 1914. The heir to the throne of the Austro-Hungarian Empire and the Duchess fell dead from an assassin's bullets while visiting the ancient city of Sarajevo, Bosnia.

Struggling with his captors, Gavrilo Princip, who killed Franz Ferdinand and Duchess Sophie, is dragged away by police and civilians, moments after the shootings which sparked the First World War.

Sarajevo, the capital of Bosnia and a province in the Austro-Hungarian Empire, was bedecked with flags and bunting on Sunday, June 28, 1914. The day was bright; the skies were clear and cloudless, and a pleasant summer's breeze wafted through the twisting cobble stone streets of the ancient city.

It should have been a festive time in Sarajevo. The authorities had declared a holiday. On every wall and fence placards urged all the townspeople to welcome the heir to the Austrian throne, the Archduke Ferdinand, and his wife, the Duchess Sophie. A ceremony was planned at the town hall and other gala events were scheduled throughout the day.

The people of Sarajevo—like all Bosnians—bore no love for the Archduke, the nephew of Emperor Franz Josef, the aged monarch who had ruled Austria-Hungary since 1848. The Bosnians regarded Archduke Ferdinand as a symbol of the hated Austrian tyranny which had torn them from Serbia, their mother country.

Discontent rumbled through Bosnia and many youths belonged to terrorist groups which vowed that one day Bosnia would be reunited with Serbia. The crowds lining Appel Quay, a narrow street which ran along the river Milica and through Sarajevo, stood in cold silence as a motorcade of open touring cars rolled past. In one, sat the Archduke and his wife. They nodded and waved smilingly to the onlookers who stared back hostilely.

Gaily uniformed dragoons escorted the royal car and ranks of soldiers guarded the street, but neither the horsemen nor the troops could prevent someone from throwing a hand grenade at the Archduke's automobile. The missile struck the open hood and bounced out to the pavement where it exploded, wounding several spectators and injuring two or three cavalrymen. Neither Ferdinand nor Sophie was hurt.

The procession sped to the city hall where the elaborate ceremonies were cut short so that the visitors could be hurried off to the safety of the palace outside the city.

The church steeple clocks were sounding noon when Ferdinand and his wife departed. Their route brought them back on the Appel Quay. The chauffeur momentarily slowed the vehicle at a street crossing. Suddenly a poorly dressed young man darted out of the crowd past soldiers and escort. Reaching the car, he yanked a Browning automatic pistol from his pocket and emptied the magazine at the Archduke and Duchess. Both fell dead under the hail of bullets.

Police, guards, onlookers and soldiers seized the assassin, an eighteen-year-old Serbian student named Gavrilo Princip, who had hoped by this drastic act to liberate Bosnia from Austria. Instead he gave the excuse for starting World War I. . . .

Aged Emperor Franz Josef had ruled the dual kingdom of Austria and Hungary since 1848 at the time his nephew and successor Archduke Franz Ferdinand was murdered.

THE UPHEAVAL
1914-1916

Map shows the railroads, rivers and roads of Serbia. The rugged terrain of the tiny country and its smaller neighbor, Montenegro, presented formidable obstacles for an invader when added to the fighting qualities of the tough Serbian and Montenegrin soldiers.

As the war clouds gathered, the task of punishing Serbia for the Archduke's death fell on the Austrian General Conrad von Hotzendorf, who was numbered among Europe's ablest soldiers.

1914

The double slaying in Sarajevo set into motion a chain of events that culminated in a four-year-long, worldwide agony that eventually involved thirty nations in the greatest war ever known up to that time.

Austrian reaction to the Archduke's death was one of vengeance; Emperor Franz Josef demanded retribution for his nephew's murder. His foreign minister, Count Leopold von Berchtold, blamed Serbia for the killings and, after receiving German assurance of support in case of war, sent Serbia a strong ultimatum on July 25.

The terms of the Austrian notes were so harsh that no one believed Serbia would accept; however, the Serbs, reluctant to fight Austria, agreed to almost everything. Field Marshal Radomir Putnik, head of Serbia's tough Army, convinced that war was imminent, ordered mobilization even as the conciliatory Serbian reply reached Vienna.

The Germans urged Emperor Franz Josef to attack Serbia. "Get it over quickly," a Berlin official advised. Austrian troops were rushed to the Serbian border under commander-in-chief, General Conrad von Hötzendorf.

Hastily mobilized to defend Serbia against Austrian aggression were these hardy Russian troops. Brave, sturdy and loyal to the Czar, the Russian soldiers needed only good equipment and leadership to defeat any enemy. They sorely lacked both.

On July 28, 1914, a month after Sarajevo, Austria formally declared war against Serbia; a day later, Emperor Franz Josef's gunboats in the Danube River began lobbing shells into Belgrade as von Hötzendorf ordered his regiments across the Serbian frontier.

By July 30, Russia moved to support Serbia. Czar Nicholas signed a decree of general mobilization and the huge Russian army lumbered into position along the frontier. The same day, the Germans sent an ultimatum to Russia and another to France; Kaiser Wilhelm demanded that the Russians stop mobilizing immediately and, to ensure French neutrality in a Russo-German War, demanded that France give over as a guarantee their fortresses at Toul and Verdun. This arrogant imposition was angrily turned down by Paris and within hours the French army was ordered to begin general mobilization.

The tensions rose in Europe; now everyone realized that war was fast becoming a reality. When the Czar refused to cancel his orders for mobilization, the Germans declared war on August 1, and that night illegally invaded the tiny Duchy of Luxembourg to seize the railheads and depots they needed for troop transport in the West.

The avalanche could no longer be stopped. On August 3, the Germans declared war against France and demanded free passage through Belgium for their troops. The Kaiser's generals believed the Belgians would not dare resist; but they had failed to reckon with the courage of King Albert I, of Belgium.

Because his country's neutrality was jointly guaranteed by a treaty which Germany, Austria, Hungary, Great Britain, France and Russia had signed, Albert rejected the Germans and mobilized his small army.

On August 4, twelve regiments of German Uhlans crossed the Belgian border near Liege; Albert's soldiers opened fire on them and hostilities began in the West.

King Albert appealed to France and Britain for help; the French were already at war with Germany and the British hesitated only a little longer. German Chancellor Theobald von Bethmann-Hollweg was advised by the British Ambassador in Berlin that unless all German troops were withdrawn from Belgium by midnight of August 4, England would declare war on Germany for violating the Belgian neutrality treaty.

"What?" the German Chancellor purportedly cried, "would you go to war over a scrap of paper?"

A solemn pledge might have been only a scrap

The finest military machine in the world was the German army, and its pride was the splendid troops of the Imperial Guard here seen passing in review before Kaiser Wilhelm and his generals.

9

(Left) Events moved swiftly in Europe during the summer of 1914. By the end of July, war was inevitable. Citizens of Paris gather around a bulletin board to read posted mobilization orders.

(Center) By August 3 Germany and France were at war. Many American residents of Paris rushed to join the French Army. A group of them march to the recruiting office behind the Stars and Stripes.

(Above) The young American poet, Alan Seegar, was one of the first to volunteer for the French Foreign Legion. The author of the poem I Have A Rendezvous With Death was killed in action in 1916.

(Left) French reservists wearing the traditional red trousers of the infantryman are given a joyous farewell as they march off to war. No one yet seemed to realize the grim ordeal ahead. War was still a grand adventure to soldiers and civilians alike.

The Germans demanded free passage for their troops through Belgium, but they were refused by King Albert who warned that his people would fight any violation of their territory.

of paper to the German government; to the British it was a commitment which had to be honorably fulfilled. At one minute past midnight, the sands had run through; King George signed the order mobilizing the armed might of the British Empire and England was at war.

In the melancholy words of the British Foreign Minister, Sir Edward Grey, Viscount of Fallodon: "The lamps are going out all over Europe; we shall not see them lit again in our lifetime. . . ."

That first week in August, 1914, when Europe went to war, the temperature reached 90 degrees Fahrenheit on the continent. However, neither the heat nor the awful reality that the long-threatened war had actually come stifled the enthusiasm and avid patriotism with which the people of the belligerents went off to fight.

Everyone believed the war would be a short one; Frenchmen and Serbs, Germans and Russians, Britons, Austrians, Belgians and Hungarians rushed eagerly to the colors, certain that God and justice were on their side. In no country was there any opposition to war; French and German socialists who had been agitating for years against "imperialistic war" threw aside their radicalism and waved the national flag, not the red banner of internationalism. Singing crowds marched through the streets of Paris, Berlin, Brussels, St. Petersburg (soon to be called Petrograd), Vienna, Budapest and London. Trainloads of troops sped to frontier po-

sitions; the men were garlanded with flowers and at each station crowds greeted them with cheers and gifts.

"*A Berlin!*" the mobs shouted in Paris—"On to Berlin!"

"*Nach Paris!*" roared Berlin's masses—"On to Paris!"

At its outset the war released a spirit of carnival jubilation. No man understood the forces that were about to be released—not the generals, the soldiers or the people who so willingly welcomed war.

The young men accepted the war eagerly; it was a chance for glory and adventure, a release from the hum-drum of daily routine. In England, which had no conscription, volunteers swamped recruiting offices, anxious to don a uniform before the war ended. ("It won't last six months," a London journalist predicted.)

Scores of American expatriates living in France enlisted in the French Foreign Legion and Parisians cheered a group of those volunteers who marched off to the railroad station bearing aloft the Stars and Stripes.

Despite the fervor and the ardor, only the Germans were trained to fight a modern war. They had Maxim machine guns and rapid-fire rifles. The Kaiser's army wore a uniform *felden-grau* (field gray) in color; the gray-green hue blended into foliage and earth making difficult targets of individual soldiers.

The French in 1914, however, still wore the red trousers, blue jackets and bright *kepis* of the Franco-Prussian War. The garish uniforms offered an easy mark for German riflemen and gunners.

The French Army's uniforms were old-fashioned and so was its tactics. Where the Germans relied on machine guns and heavy artillery, the French depended upon the bayonet. The philosophy of France's military

Sir Edward Grey, England's Secretary of State for Foreign Affairs, understood the tragedy that had fallen upon the world. On August 4, when England declared war against Germany, Grey uttered his famous remark: "The lamps are going out all over Europe; we shall not see them lit again in our lifetime."

Theobald von Bethmann-Hollweg, the German Chancellor, upon learning that England would stand by the treaty guaranteeing Belgian neutrality, cried out to the English Ambassador, "What? Would you go to war over a scrap of paper?"

leadership was the *offensive à outrance*—attack to the utmost—in the mistaken belief that no troops in the world could stand up to a French infantry bayonet charge.

Even General Joseph Joffre, the French commander-in-chief, a capable and intelligent officer, failed to realize that a comparatively few men behind machine guns could annihilate any infantry charge. In fact, the French military minds understood very little about 20th-century warfare, particularly the brand displayed by the Germans. . . .

The first to feel the brunt of German might were men like these quaintly uniformed Belgian soldiers (top, right) here forming a skirmish line against advancing German Uhlans—the Kaiser's crack mounted troops.

Although outnumbered and outclassed, the brave Belgians contested every inch of their land. This drawing (center) portrays a hot hand-to-hand fight as the Germans sought to cross the Yser Canal.

Brushing aside all resistance, the huge German army rolls through the Belgian countryside, field kitchens carrying hot food to the forward units (right). Note lance-bearing Uhlans at the right.

By August 6, help was at hand for the embattled Belgians. Spirited, disciplined British Royal Marines were among the first to arrive. Citizens of Ostend give them a rousing reception as the Marines trod the cobbled street.

Clad in uniforms more suitable for war in 1870, not 1914, French infantrymen attack with their favorite weapon—the bayonet. Despite their dash and courage, troops such as these were no match for the machine guns and rapid-firing rifles of the Germans.

Just as the Kaiser's expansionist ambitions had been known throughout Europe, so was his main plan for military conquest in the West—a scheme known as the "Schlieffen Plan," for General Alfred von Schlieffen, the German Chief of Staff, which called for a flanking movement of the French by vast German forces through southeastern Holland and Belgium.

"Keep the right wing strong," von Schlieffen emphasized. He wanted to swing so wide through Belgium that the last man on the right would "brush the English Channel with his sleeve."

With this maneuver, von Schlieffen proposed to outflank the French fortified positions on the German frontier. The French defensive positions and forts between Belfort and Verdun, he believed, were "impregnable." Only by marching into Holland and Belgium could the French fortresses be rendered worthless, von Schlieffen emphasized.

Von Schlieffen had based his plan on the propo-

Cannon such as this giant Austrian-made howitzer, manufactured at the Skoda Plant, were hauled to the Western Front, where they soon smashed the bravely defended Belgian forts at Liege and Namur.

Portly General Joseph Joffre, known as "Pappa" by his soldiers, confers with dapper General Ferdinand Foch, one of his chief subordinates. At the outbreak of the war, Pappa Joffre was Commander in Chief of the French Army. Four years later, Foch led all the Allied armies to victory as Supreme Commander.

sition that Germany would have to fight on two fronts; that Russia would hurl her masses against Germany's eastern borders. In addition, von Schlieffen anticipated British intervention and the presence of British troops on the continent.

He was hardly concerned with the British. "We will gather them up like so many rabbits," he boasted. As for the Russians, von Schlieffen again seemed little bothered. "It matters little what they do. We will attend to the Russians once we destroy the French," he said.

Only the French Army mattered to von Schlieffen. He intended to deal with it swiftly. The elaborate German time-table called for a six-week campaign—a *blitzkrieg* or lightning war.

Again, he was not concerned with what the enemy would do. Well aware that French strategy called for an offensive into Alsace-Lorraine at the

start of a conflict with Germany, von Schlieffen proposed defensive action against both French and Russian assaults at the same time unloosing his main power against Holland, Belgium and France.

The key to German victory lay in keeping the right wing overwhelmingly strong and striking speedily in an onslaught so massive that nothing could stop or slow it.

History might have been written differently had von Schlieffen's Plan been carried out to the letter. He died in 1912, at the age of 80. His successor as chief of the general staff was General Helmuth von Moltke, nephew and namesake of the soldier who had humbled France in 1870-1871.

However, the von Moltke of 1914 was no military genius; he resembled his uncle in name only. The new chief of staff was a worrier; no sooner had he replaced von Schlieffen than he tampered with the Plan. The invasion of Holland was dropped, because von Moltke feared the Dutch would flood their land to impede the Germans and slow down the *blitzkrieg*.

Von Moltke also sent more troops to the Eastern Front; he did not have the nerve required to let the Russians invade German soil. The thought that a major breakthrough might occur haunted him day and night; for this reason, von Moltke ordered additional divisions from the vital right wing to reinforce the Alsace-Lorraine frontier.

These changes doomed the Schlieffen Plan. Even if von Moltke had not tampered with it, no planners or strategists could have foreseen the epic resistance of the Belgians, or that the British Army—which Kaiser Wilhelm had once described as "a contemptible little army" and which von Schlieffen planned to gather up "like so many rabbits"—would prove to consist of lions.

Von Moltke's armies struck at Liege and Namur in Belgium. The forts guarding these vital points were

Map (top) illustrates the four-pronged German assault, a modification of the famed von Schlieffen Plan, which called for a swing through southern Holland and the capture of the Channel ports.

Spike-helmeted Field Marshal Graf Helmuth von Moltke (center) led the Kaiser's armies in 1914. His alteration of the von Schlieffen Plan ended all chance of speedy German victory and brought about four bloody years of vicious trench warfare on the Western Front.

Gruff Field Marshal Sir John French (left) led the British Expeditionary Force (B.E.F.) to France and Belgium in August, 1914. A hero of the Boer War, Sir John never quite grasped the complexities of modern warfare. In December, 1915, he was relieved by Field Marshal Sir Douglas Haig.

obsolete, capable of withstanding 8-inch shells but nothing bigger. However, the Germans had not brought up the heavy Krupp and Skoda 17-inch siege guns with which to batter the forts.

Although the city of Liege itself fell during the night of August 5, it took the Germans ten days to capture the forts, after rushing their biggest cannon to the front. Namur, the last bastion standing between the invaders and France, was smashed into submission by August 23.

Meanwhile, the French had engaged the enemy in a series of bloody clashes known as the Battles of the Frontiers. They lasted from August 14-25 and cost the French more than 300,000 casualties. The losses had mounted that high because of the stubborn insistence with which the French relied upon the bayonet; even the Germans were appalled at the slaughter wrought by their machine guns. For a brief time French troops won a foothold in Alsace-Lorraine, but the moral victory was not worth the sacrifice in men and equipment. A German counter-attack drove out Joffre's men and the French threat in Alsace was ended.

Three surviving gunners of "L" Battery, Royal Horse Artillery, tend their piece during the Battle of Mons where 30,000 men of the B.E.F. fought the Germans to a standstill on August 23.

General Joffre, who was called "Pappa" by his troops because he resembled a benign father rather than a soldier, did not recognize the full danger of the German offensive in Belgium. Not until August 21, did he realize that the foe was actually carrying through the Schlieffen Plan, although he had been warned since the first days of the German invasion. Now, almost too late, he started rushing troops northward to check the Germans.

Also marching to meet the oncoming enemy was a British Expeditionary Force of 150,000 men commanded by General Sir John French. The British force had been landed on August 7 at Ostend, Calais and Dunkirk. As yet the "Old Contemptibles," as the British regulars called themselves, referring to Kaiser Wilhelm's description of the British Army, had not been in action.

Fast-marching German troops stream through Amiens, France, on the road to Paris, during the latter part of August, 1914. A handful of the city's residents watch the invaders pass.

Be-medalled General Alexander von Kluck (right), commanding the First German Army in Belgium and France. The Second German Army, commanded by General Karl von Bulow (left), worked in close cooperation with von Kluck to smash through Belgian defenses at Liege.

Miracle at the Marne

About 30,000 men of the B.E.F. were concentrated at Mons on August 23, directly in the path of the German First Army under General Alexander von Kluck. Some 90,000 Germans attacked the British positions and, for the first time in almost a month of fighting, von Kluck's troops were stopped short.

The rifle fire of the "Old Contemptibles" was so devastating that startled German intelligence officers reported the enemy had 28 machine guns per battalion. This was news to the British; they had only two automatic weapons in each battalion. The Germans had simply not previously encountered troops whose skill, discipline and training was superior to theirs.

However, the British were forced to fall back under the weight of numbers. They withdrew to Le Cateau and fought another bruising rear guard action on August 26, checking the Germans long enough to permit an orderly retreat to the Marne River line where Joffre ordered a last ditch stand. *"Ils ne passeront pas!"* —"they shall not pass!"—chanted the French reserves marching up to the front.

Behind the lines, Paris was readied for a siege. A tough old regular, General Joseph Galliéni, was made military governor of the city; the government moved to Bordeaux and the capital became an armed camp. Troops were everywhere, barricades blocked the streets, and every able-bodied citizen was mobilized either for digging entrenchments or carrying a weapon.

All over France, people crowded the churches to pray for Divine help to halt the *boches*. They pleaded for a miracle, but the Germans still came relentlessly on. . . .

The miracle for which the French had been entreating took place along the banks of the Marne River where the most decisive battle of the First World War was fought from September 5-12 inclusively. On the 5th, French units crashed headlong into advance elements of von Kluck's army, and a tremendous struggle developed. Galliéni, making astute use of aircraft for reconnaissance purposes, found a place to hit the Germans on the flank and did so effectively.

A gap was opened between the German 1st Army (von Kluck) and the 2nd (von Bülow). British and French troops slammed into the gap and widened it. When frontline units needed reinforcements on September 7-8, Galliéni rushed two regiments forward in Parisian taxis.

The fighting was nip-and-tuck. German mounted scouts reached a point where they could see the spire of the Eiffel Tower on the horizon fourteen miles away. The French were determined to check the enemy or die. During one crucial phase of the battle, General Ferdinand Foch, commanding the 9th Army, sent a dispatch to Joffre:

> *"Hard pressed on my right. My center is yielding. Impossible to maneuver. Situation excellent, I attack!"*

Such spirit was not to be denied. On September 12, the Germans withdrew to the Aisne River. General von Moltke, shaken by the defeat, reported gloomily to the Kaiser, "Sire, we have lost the war!"

These were indeed prophetic words. Germany had lost the war—but it was to take millions of lives,

During the first week in September, the situation grew critical for the French. Both von Kluck and von Bulow were at the Marne River; German advanced patrols could see the spires of Paris only twenty miles away. The city was in command of hardy General Joseph Gallieni and he prepared Paris for defense. The "City of Light" became a fortress with barricades on every street corner.

French soldiers such as these seven infantrymen were rushed to the Marne in Paris taxicabs. They halted the Germans in desperate fighting. This action photograph shows the tense squad moments after taking an enemy position.

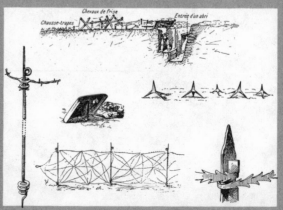

(Left) *Dead Germans lie sprawled in a trench after a French bayonet charge. This picture of an incident in the Marne fighting starkly illustrates war's grimness. The victors are almost obscured by the morning mists. At the left, one young soldier stares with distaste at the enemy corpses.*

Three Germans (right) entered the city of Soissons one rainy morning in September. Perhaps they thought it was held by their men. Sentries shot them down in the square and the war was over for these invaders of France.

vast sums of money and four hideous years before von Moltke's Cassandra-like utterance came to pass. The Kaiser lost faith in von Moltke, and on September 14 the chief of the general staff was replaced by General Erich von Falkenhayn. The announced reason for von Moltke's replacement was poor health, but it was no secret that failure on the Marne brought about his downfall.

The day of the *blitzkrieg* in the West had ended. Except for a series of battles known as "The Race To The Sea," in which each side tried to outflank the other as the Germans tried to gain control of the Channel coast, the war of movement had ended also. They succeeded only in capturing Antwerp which the Belgians defended valiantly until October 9 and then skillfully evacuated, bringing out the most intact the gallant field army which had fought so bravely against incredible odds.

King Albert clung to a tiny corner of his country until the end of the war and the long, arduous ordeal of trench warfare began. A final bloody struggle, known to history as the First Battle of Ypres, took place from October 12 until November 11 in the mud of Flanders. There the "Old Contemptibles" proved for all time how Britain could fight. Never again would the Germans be contemptuous of the British Army.

Now, the Western Front became a thousand-mile-long series of trenches and barbed wire entanglements. The whole nature of warfare changed. A new arsenal of weapons was needed; the hand grenade, the trench mortar, the high-explosive shell, the machine gun and the rifle became the major weapons. Horse cavalry, which had dominated battlefields for centuries, was rendered obsolete forever; no more would mounted men ride in thundering charges to rout the foe with lance and saber. The day of glory in war was ended. It now became only mud, blood, death and suffering.

Never in history had so many been killed, maimed and wounded in such a short time. At the close of 1914, more than 854,000 Frenchmen had shed their blood for *La Patrie* and a total of 677,000 Germans had fallen for *Der Vaterland,* while the brave B.E.F. lost 75,000 men of the original 150,000 who had gone to serve God, King and Country.

Weapons such as the machine gun, hand grenade and magazine rifle came into extensive use at the beginning of World War I. Trench mortars, various types of barbed wire and other defensive devices were also employed. The rifles of the belligerent armies are shown at the right.

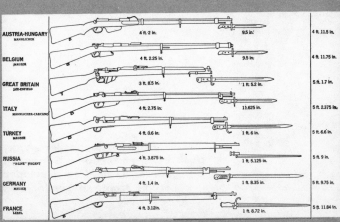

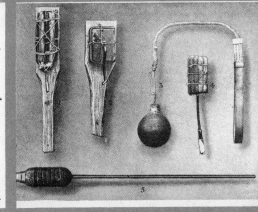

Bayonets to the fore, crack Russian troops pass in review before leaving for the front. Men such as these gave a good account of themselves in the early days of the war.

Fury in the East

Czar Nicholas II and the Grand Duke Nicholas, his uncle, meet at the front. The Duke, who stood nearly seven feet tall, commanded Russian forces in the field.

Drawing (opposite) vividly depicts a frontier clash between invading Germans and Russian border guards. As fighting developed along the Eastern Front, scores of similar skirmishes took place.

As the slaughter was raging in the West, the Eastern Front flamed. On August 17, 200,000 Russians launched an offensive against the 150,000-man German Army in East Prussia, but the attack was ineptly handled. The common Russian soldier lacked neither courage nor endurance; he suffered instead from a scarcity of artillery, modern weapons and capable leaders.

The "Russian Steamroller" lurched slowly into East Prussia but by August 27 ran into difficulty at Tannenberg, where a German counter-offensive that lasted until August 30 literally destroyed a Russian Army. General Erich von Ludendorff who led the German stroke repeated that performance at the Masurian Lakes ten days later. In about a month's fighting, the Russians lost in killed, wounded and captured almost 150,000 of the 200,000 men who had started the invasion of East Prussia. In addition to inflicting ghastly casualties on the Czarist army, the Germans captured

650 pieces of artillery, a severe blow to the Russians who had only 5,000 field guns altogether.

Against the Austrians, farther south on the vast Eastern Front, the Russians had far better luck. In the first place, thousands of Austro-Hungarian troops were Slavs and Czechs who looked to the Russians as blood-brothers. They had suffered persecution and discrimination under the rule of Emperor Franz Josef and were not inclined to fight hard for a despotic monarch; consequently, many deserted to the Russians at the first chance. In addition, the Austrian High Command blundered by attacking headlong across the Polish border in a bid to capture Warsaw. These troops were caught in the open by a Russian army of over-

Fierce Cossack horsemen overrun enemy positions somewhere in the Eastern war zone (above). Heavy rainfalls turned Galicia into a quagmire which Russians nicknamed "General Mud."

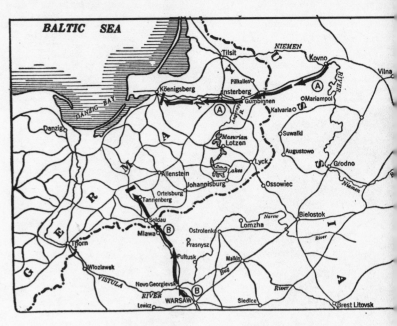

whelming numbers; in the series of battles-that followed, the Austrians were all but annihilated.

They fled in pell-mell retreat and the Russians swiftly overran most of Galicia. However, the Austrians managed to form a line at the Wisloka River and with the help of hastily mobilized German reinforcements managed to hold off the Russians. Furious fighting raged until the end of the year, with the line see-sawing back and forth while cities changed hands a half dozen times.

The hapless Austrians also suffered a mauling at the hands of the tough Serbian Army commanded by wily Field Marshal Radomir Putnik. The Austrians had attacked in Serbia at the outbreak of war only to be ignominiously beaten at the Drina River in a twelve-day struggle that lasted from August 12-24. Humiliated, the Austrians made an all-out effort to crush the Serbs and succeeded in taking Belgrade by December 2 after weeks of gruelling mountain warfare. But the Serbs were not yet finished. In a desperate counter-attack that started December 3, they routed the Austrians, recapturing Belgrade on December 16 and driving the enemy before them in total defeat.

The victory was a costly one for the tiny Serbian Army; they lost 100,000 men in killed, wounded, captured or missing. The Austrians took equally heavy casualties.

The situation on the Eastern Front, by the end of 1914, was apparently not unfavorable to the Allies. Although the Germans had beaten the Russians decisively at Tannenberg and the Masurian Lakes, Russian victories over the Austrians made up for the defeats. However, the material losses in weapons and equipment lost by Russia almost paralyzed the Czar's armies.

With the war on the Western Front bogged down in the stalemate of trench warfare, the Germans were enabled to release thousands of troops for service

(Above) On August 31, 1914, the Russians suffered a shattering defeat at Tannenberg (B). This caused them to withdraw from East Prussia where a Czarist Army under General Pavel Rennenkampf had captured the important German city of Koenigsberg (A). Thousands of Russians were killed, wounded or captured at Tannenberg.

General Erich von Ludendorff (above, left,) one of the top German commanders at the Battle of Tannenberg, was teamed with General Paul von Hindenburg (center). Probably the greatest of the German staff officers, von Hindenburg would emerge from the war as Germany's most beloved national hero.

Numberless Russians file past in sway-backed columns after their capture at Tannenberg. It was estimated that more than 125,000 of them fell into the neatly sprung trap which von Hindenburg and von Ludendorff had prepared for them.

Somewhere on the vast Eastern Front, the timeless tragedy of war is re-enacted when beshawled women return to their ruined homes and futilely search for treasured belongings after the battle has swept past.

Russian walking wounded trudge toward German field hospital after the catastrophe of Tannenberg. Officers and men alike were carried away in the tidal wave of total defeat.

Hard-fighting Serbs in hastily dug trench
are reinforced by a fresh detachment as they
prepare to meet the onslaught of their
better-armed Austrian foes.

against Russia. Also, Turkey had entered the war on the side of Germany at the end of October. This created new problems for Russia. The Dardanelles-Black Sea route was closed to Allied shipping; Russia was practically isolated from Great Britain and France.

The Russian supply shortage, always acute, became precarious at the end of 1914. Unless the Allies found some way to re-equip the Czar's armies, the future was a bleak one for Russia. Although her brave soldiers were loyal and devoted to the Czar, whom they called "Little Father," and the stolid peasant-soldiers were still willing to die for "Holy Mother Russia," they could not fight without weapons. Certain British leaders, such as First Admiralty Lord Winston Churchill, gave much thought to helping Russia. Early in 1915, he hit upon a scheme which he persuaded other influential French and British officials would prove effective.

Gruesome sights such as this were
commonplace in Serbia where the Austrians pushed
slowly forward. Austrian commanders treated
Serbs with great cruelty. Here, the bodies of youths
13 to 16, accused of sniping at Austrian troops,
lie in a field. The enemy forced their relatives (background) to look upon the ugly scene.

1915

Gallipoli—Bold Failure

(Right) On March 18, 1915, victory seemed within the grasp of the Allied navy. The Turkish batteries had been silenced and the way through the Dardanelles opened. Only a few enemy mines blocked the passage. Unhappily, several Allied warships struck mines, among them the H.M.S. Irresistible, shown here in a sinking condition, and the naval forces withdrew.

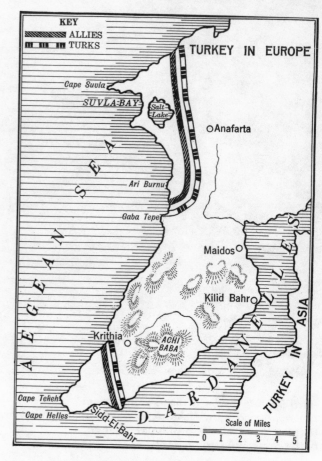

Map of the Gallipoli Peninsula shows the Allied and Turkish battle lines and the strategic, winding Dardanelles, the gateway to the Near East.

The British warship H.M.S. Albion (below) under fire from the guns of the Turkish forts in February, 1915, as the bombardment of the Dardanelles defenses was begun by a Franco-British fleet.

Winston S. Churchill, England's First Lord of the Admiralty, conceived the daring plan to force the Dardanelles, thus launching the ill-fated Gallipoli Campaign.

The idea conceived by Churchill was to have strong French and British naval squadrons blast through the Dardanelles, a narrow-winding channel that led to Constantinople, the capital of Turkey, via the Sea of Marmara; from the Turkish capital, the route went on into the Black Sea and the Russian port of Odessa.

Churchill's plan was highly feasible. The Turks were weak and had been more hindrance than help to the Germans. The Turkish Army of about 500,000 men had been unsuccessful in Mesopotamia, Persia, Palestine and on the Russian Front; between November, 1914, and January, 1915, a whole Turkish corps was destroyed by the Russians in the snow-capped Caucasus Mountains.

Churchill and his supporters believed a determined assault might knock Turkey out of the war, but they saw beyond that immediate benefit. A triumph over Turkey, besides opening a direct and accessible supply line to Russia, had the possibility of turning wavering neutrals such as Greece, Bulgaria, Rumania and Italy against Germany and Austria-Hungary. Each of these countries had territorial claims against the Austro-Hungarian Empire. A combined attack would have overthrown the teetering regime of Franz Josef. Without a major ally, Germany could not long endure; the proponents of the Dardanelles venture predicted that success in the operation would mean a victorious end to the war by 1916.

Forcing the Dardanelles presented a tough prob-lem, but not an insuperable one. Although many Turkish forts guarded the passage, the bastions were old, their guns obsolete and no match for the big calibre cannon of battleships. However, the Turks had mounted field artillery and howitzers at strategic points. The entrance to the Dardanelles (known as The Narrows) and the channel itself were strewn with strings of mines.

After much argument, Churchill persuaded the Allied military and naval commanders to give support to his project. By February 19, a Franco-British fleet was lying off the entrance to the Dardanelles and bombarding the enemy forts. The shelling by the ships battered many of the Turkish forts into submission. By March 18, the Allied fleet began moving through the channel behind mine sweepers. Unhappily for the British and French, the mine sweepers were mishandled and the job was bungled. A number of mines were left intact and after two French and two British vessels were blown up, the naval force was withdrawn.

The Turks watched the retreat in amazement; they were nearly out of ammunition, their forts were smashed, their gun positions destroyed. "Another day and we would have been forced to yield," a Turkish spokesman declared.

Although scores of British and French sailors volunteered to take the mine sweepers back again and do a proper job, the naval attack was never renewed. Instead, a haphazard plan to capture the Gallipoli Penin-

sula, which flanked the Dardanelles, was adopted. Seldom has a major military operation been so badly conducted. The landings which began on April 25 were botched, openings missed, and opportunities for victory thrown away.

Only the sheer courage of the Australian and New Zealand Army Corps (ANZAC), the grit of the common soldier, and the stubborn fighting qualities displayed by British and French troops prevented Gallipoli from turning into disaster. The enlisted men and junior officers rose to the challenge, but were let down by the High Command.

The Turks under German General Liman von Sanders and Mustafa Kemal fought skillfully and bravely. At last, the British pulled out of Gallipoli when the realization came that stupidity was leading to a debacle. The Gallipoli evacuation was carried out with brilliance and imagination; not until the last man was on ship did

Battlefield artist shows landing of Australian and New Zealand corps (ANZAC) at Gaba Tepe on Gallipoli Peninsula, April 25, 1915. Shells from Turkish batteries on the heights splash amidst the landing barges and other vessels. Note columns of infantry moving off the beach.

General Sir Ian Hamilton (left), commanding the British forces on Gallipoli, handled his courageous troops so ineptly that many chances for total victory were wasted.

A view of a landing beach at Gallipoli (above) underlines the desolate terrain. This ANZAC beachhead is limited in space for storing supplies, while the rocky ledges provide little shelter for the men. Seldom have troops endured the hardships suffered by those who fought in the Gallipoli Campaign. German General Liman von Sanders (left) organized and led the Turkish and German forces which successfully defended Gallipoli against the invading Allies.

Transports disembark British troops under fire while warships in the background pound the shoreline with their big guns.

Under the pitiless glare of a blistering sun a British army camp bakes in the waterless wastes of arid Gallipoli (left). With the Turks holding the heights, the British could make no unobserved movements and were constantly under enemy artillery fire.

Front-line artist captures tense moment when the last Allied troops made a brilliant withdrawal from Gallipoli under enemy guns. Fires on shore are from burning military supplies which could not be removed. The costly, tragic struggle at Gallipoli was lost through Allied blunders and stupidity. The only part of the operation handled skillfully was the evacuation.

Photograph shows Austrian Alpine troops making a perilous ascent to outflank enemy mountain positions.

the Turks realize that the foe had withdrawn.

"If the whole affair had been conducted as well as the retreat," wrote a British journalist, "we'd have been in Constantinople months ago."

The venture had been expensive. Of the 489,000 Allied troops engaged, some 252,000 became casualties. About 500,000 Turks were in the action and some 250,000 were killed, captured, wounded or missing.

The Gallipoli Campaign had some side-effects for the Allies. Although Italy had entered the war against Austria and Germany on April 26 (the day after the first landings at Gallipoli), the Anglo-French failure to take the Peninsula convinced wavering Bulgaria to join the Central Powers (Germany, Austria-Hungary and Turkey).

In September, 1915, the Bulgars, reinforced by Austro-German troops, launched a crushing attack against Serbia. The hardy Serbs resisted to the last but were finally crushed in December. The Serbian Army made an epic retreat across the mountains to Albania where French and Italian ships carried them to Corfu for rest, recuperation and the chance to fight again. . . .

The day after the landings at Gallipoli, Italy finally cast its lot with England and France, and the Italians were soon engaged in heavy fighting against the Austrians.

Steel-helmeted Italian infantry (below) charge through Austrian barbed wire in a perilous dash across the rocky No Man's Land that separates them from the enemy's lines.

In September, 1915, Czar Ferdinand of Bulgaria (left) threw the Bulgarian army against the embattled Serbs who were already outnumbered by their Austro-German foes. An emaciated and ragged Serbian soldier (right) poses for a picture after escaping across the mountains to Albania. Along with thousands of his countrymen, this survivor was transported to the Isle of Corfu, and re-equipped to fight again.

Bulgarian infantry (above) advances across a grassy slope toward Serbian positions. Note shells bursting in the background. They signal the commencement of a heavy Serb barrage concentrated against the Bulgars.

In this tragic scene, King Peter (seated, below), the aged ruler of Serbia, looks back at his lost kingdom as Germans, Austrians and Bulgarians overrun the land.

Sacrifice, Slaughter and Stalemate in the West

The long-range strategy of Gallipoli was beyond the thinking capacities of the Allied military chiefs in France and Belgium. The generals had either derided, scorned or ignored the effort at Gallipoli. "It was all waste and nonsense. The war can be won only in France. The *boches* has committed himself here and it is here we shall destroy him," a high-ranking British officer stated.

The tactic chosen to destroy the *boches* was one more suitable for 19th-century battlefields than 20th-century warfare. In March, both Pappa Joffre and Sir John French were still determined to break through the German lines by massive frontal assaults. They decided upon a "war of attrition"—that is, to keep attacking the enemy until he had exhausted his manpower.

"The only thing wrong with that logic," an American observer wrote, "is that you might run out of men before the foe did. . . ."

The gruesome horrors of trench war daily became more ghastly as the spring offensives got under way. During March, French troops hurled themselves in reckless assaults against the entrenched Germans in Champagne and at the St. Mihiel salient near Verdun. The Germans, well dug-in, sat behind their machine guns and ripped the attackers to shreds. That same month, Sir John French sent the remnants of the B.E.F. to disaster at Neuve Chapelle. The soil of Northern France was soggy with blood as casualties mounted to sickening totals.

During April, the Germans came up with a weapon which might well have won the war for them had it been properly employed on a large scale. On April 22, a splendid spring day, the Allied lines in the Ypres section were subjected to severe shelling.

At 5:00 P.M., the Germans made military history; they released clouds of greenish-yellow chlorine gas from more than 5,000 cylinders. The deadly fog was swept by the breeze onto the Franco-British trenches. Men fled, choking and gasping as the poisonous fumes swirled around them. A gap was opened in the French line; the way was clear for a German breakthrough, but the Germans were wary of their own weapons and advanced cautiously.

"Pappa" Joffre sent his men against the Germans in the Champagne (right) as spring came to France in 1915. Furious French bayonet attacks such as this were bloodily repulsed by the Kaiser's troops. British commander, Sir John French, hurled the brave men of the B.E.F. (below) at the Germans in futile frontal assaults in Northern France.

They went forward so timidly that the British plugged the hole effectively and although gas was again used by the Germans on April 24, no decisive gains were made. Soon, troops were issued masks as a defense against gas and by September, when prevailing winds blew toward the German positions, the Allies gave them a taste of chlorine.

That spring, poison gas became an established weapon in the arsenal of modern warfare. Newer and deadlier gases, such as mustard and phosgene, were added. Chemists and technicians, behind the lines, fought with test tube instead of rifles but killed the enemy as surely as a sniper's bullet.

The French and British mounted one attack after another. As summer flowers bloomed in the shell-torn dirt of Flanders and Picardy, and green shoots poked out of the devastated land, the Allied generals paused to tally their losses: from April through June they counted 300,000 casualties and only an eight-mile gain of war-ravaged territory.

In October, Sir John French sent the British First Army under Gen. Sir Douglas Haig into another abortive attack; this time in the mining region of Loos. The results were appalling—60,000 British casualties against 20,000 German. That battle marked the end of General French. On December 15, he was replaced by Sir Douglas Haig who became commander-in-chief of British troops in France.

Pappa Joffre unleashed a three-day-long artillery bombardment of 2,500 guns in another attempt to smash the Germans holding the Champagne sector. Not even that rain of shells could blast a path for Joffre's men. A terrible battle raged for the high ground of Vimy Ridge; but by mid-November Joffre called off the offensive. He had little to show for all the blood that had been shed except 150,000 men killed, wounded, missing and captured. The Germans, however, had not

Soldiers soon became hardened to war's grisly business. This detail is removing the dead and wounded from a trench after the repulse of a German counterattack.

British engineers slosh through the muddy, flooded fields of Flanders to construct the bed for a military railroad. The mud made life intolerable for the troops.

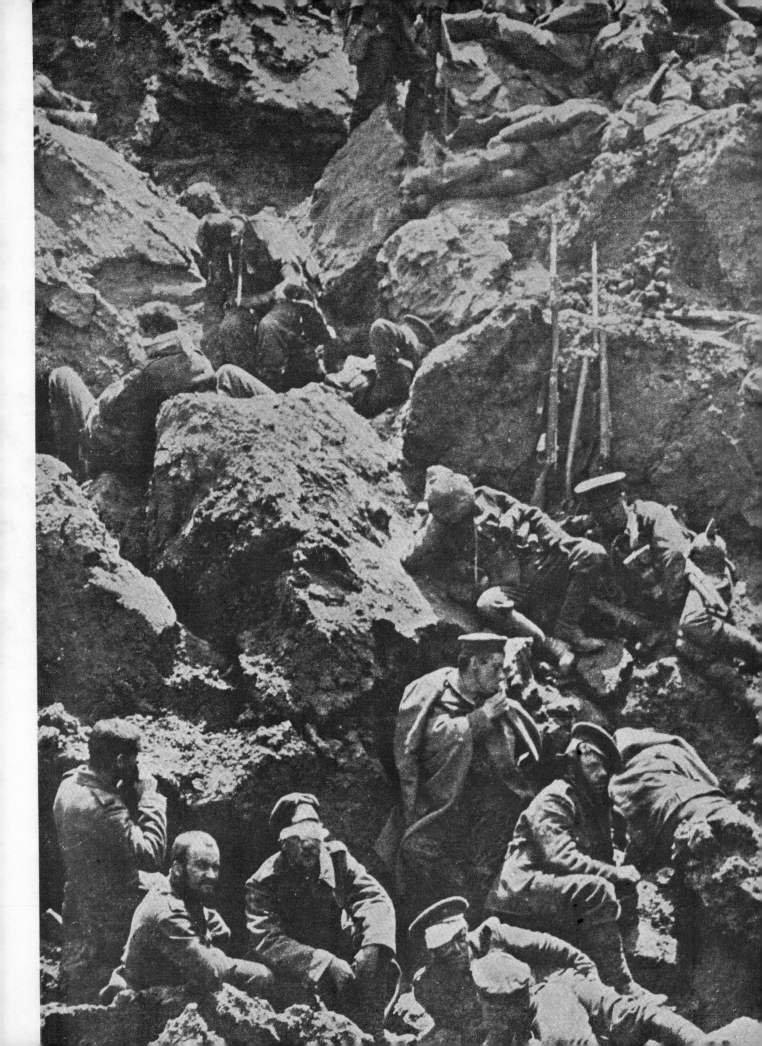

The aftermath of a mine exploded by the British under a German strong-point in Flanders. Wounded Germans, dead men and bayonet-wielding Tommies mingle in a welter of blood, mud, death and pain.

Street fighting rages in Ypres, Belgium, between British and Germans (above). Artist depicts scene during First Battle of Ypres in October, 1914. Months later, vicious battles still continued in the same sector.

One of the war's cruelest weapons was unveiled by the Germans in April, 1915. They released chlorine gas against British Tommies defending a point near Ypres. Drawing (left) illustrates violent effect of the gas on its victims. That autumn, the Germans were themselves subjected to poison gas attacks as the Allies put the deadly chemical into use.

Respirators or gas masks soon became standard equipment for all front-line soldiers. British machine gunners wearing gas masks prepare for action somewhere on the Western Front.

escaped unscathed; they paid with 100,000 casualties.

A British statesman castigated the so-called war of attrition as "mass murder." In 1915, the battlefields of France were a vast slaughterhouse where the best young manhood of Great Britain, France and Germany was wasted. Losses were staggering. More than 1,500,000 Britons and Frenchmen had fallen while the Germans mourned casualties totalling above 600,000 men. The year 1915 was a grist mill that ground-up human beings. For all the slaughter and sacrifice, the lines had not moved three miles in either direction.

Disaster in the East

The doughty German generals Paul von Hindenburg, Erich von Ludendorff and August von Mackensen planned to destroy Russian resistance in 1915 and bring the war on the Eastern Front to a successful conclusion. The chances for swift German triumph seemed to be good.

It mattered little to the German High Command that more than 6,000,000 Russians were in uniform; that huge army, German intelligence knew, was only a *papier-mâché* giant. One Russian soldier in three had no rifle; Czarist artillery lacked shells. The Russians suffered a dearth of every military necessity from horseshoes to bandages.

Yet, *l'esprit* and morale of the average Russian soldier remained high. "I will pick up a rifle on the battlefield; if I cannot find one, I shall fight with stones," a Russian soldier wrote to his family.

The almost mystical power of "The Little Father" weaved a spell over the masses that made up the Russian people, the bulk of whom were illiterate peasants, so steeped in ignorance and superstition that a Russian writer called them "The Dark People."

Although they were being used as cannon fodder, "The Dark People" retained a fanatical devotion to the Czar; however, not all Russians were enamored of their ruler. The relatively few industrial workers of Russia were indoctrinated with radical and revolutionary philosophies. Among them were Mensheviks (socialists), Bolsheviks (communists), Anarchists, Syndicalists and Nihilists.

The Russian working class had a long tradition of struggle against Czarist oppression. As recently as 1905, there had been an unsuccessful revolution aimed at overthrowing the Czar. Although many leaders of the 1905 revolt had been imprisoned or exiled to Siberia, the spirit of it still smoldered. Even in the army, the left-wing radicals kept up their agitation; not every Russian went blindly to his doom in battle.

Czar Nicholas was a weak-minded man, easily dominated by stronger willed people; he surrounded himself with inept advisers who flattered and applauded his every move. In addition to these sycophants, the Czar was greatly influenced by a strange and evil man, a bogus monk named Rasputin, who held a unique position in the royal household. Through guile and intrigue, Rasputin convinced the Czarina, a not very bright lady, that he possessed Divine healing powers and, in fact, did cure the Czarina's youngest son when the boy was very ill.

After that, Rasputin became a fixture around the palace; the Czar heeded his advice as did the Royal Ministers. Many level-headed and patriotic Russians believed Rasputin was a German agent who had wormed his way into the highest places and was daily betraying Russia. But when even a whisper of this rumor reached the Czar or the Czarina neither would listen.

Thus in the East as 1915 began, Russia, ruled by an insipid Czar, stood unprepared for the German onslaught. While the poorly equipped peasant-soldiers awaited the enemy, Rasputin lived in exotic luxury, a favored guest in court who could ruin almost anyone's career with the merest hint to the Czar or the Czarina.

And while the soldiers marched into battle without proper weapons, clothing or food, the royal family and the courtiers dined like Oriental potentates. It was said that the garbage thrown out after a single royal banquet could have fed a regiment in the field for a week.

As the wintry weather lifted, the best equipped Russian forces struck at the Austro-Hungarian troops in the Carpathian Mountains. This offensive made such swift progress that a breakthrough into the Hungarian plains seemed likely.

This moment of Russian triumph was of brief duration. On May 1, the Germans rushed to rescue the hapless Austrians. Huge cannon blasted the Russian lines near Cracow, Poland, and a furious offensive got underway. The Russians could not stop the enemy. There were Czarist troops that surrendered by regiments and divisions, while others fought bravely until annihilated.

Grigori Rasputin, who held almost hypnotic power over the Russian Czar and Czarina, used his influence at court to further his own greedy ambitions. Many patriotic Russian noblemen regarded him as a menace to the country and it was rumored that Rasputin served the Germans as a secret agent.

Despite the great losses of 1914, the Russians again took the offensive in 1915. Shown in photograph (above) is a Russian brigade on the march. Note trucks as well as pack animals hauling supplies.

Austrian troops in Galicia (right) tensely await massive Russian onslaught. Improvised trenches provide scant shelter for retreating Austrians.

On and on the Kaiser's armies pressed. By the beginning of August, the Germans took Warsaw, Vilna fell, as did Kovno, Brest-Litovsk and other important centers. As winter set in, the Germans held all of Poland and the Baltic states. Over 1,000,000 Russians had been captured and an equal number lost in battle; small wonder that von Hindenburg, von Ludendorff and von Mackensen smiled in satisfaction at the results of their grand offensive.

"Soon, our valiant soldiers will be parading in Petrograd," a Berlin war correspondent wrote. "The Russians are conquered . . . they will never recover to do battle again. . . ."

More than 100 years earlier, Napoleon had similarly misjudged the Russians. Twenty-six years later, in 1941, another generation of Germans were to make the same mistake. No man seemed to comprehend fully the tremendous will of the Russian people.

Full fury of the Russian assault forces Austro-Hungarian troops into headlong flight harrassed by Cossack cavalrymen (background).

(Below) Russian triumphs in 1915 were shortlived. The Germans bolstered flagging Austrian and Hungarian forces. Poorly equipped and badly led Russians were unable to cope with Germans and the Czar's offensive ended disastrously. Here Germans guard captive Russians.

The victorious Germans faced an even deadlier foe than the Russian army. The constant companion of war—plague—swept through areas of Poland. In this occupied town stricken by dread cholera, German medical authorities post warnings to newly arrived troops that the disease was rampant.

1916

Ordeal at Verdun

In 1916, from a German viewpoint, the war was going well. However, some flaws marred the happy picture. The British blockade had been making itself increasingly felt in Germany and Austria. Despite German military victories, food shortages were growing in the Kaiser's domain; items such as coffee, butter, eggs and medical supplies became scarcer every day.

Austria-Hungary was proving itself to be more liability than asset; Franz Josef's empire was creaking badly and his armies had to be bailed out by the Germans every time they undertook an action. Similarly, Bulgaria and Turkey were more a hindrance than a help to the Germans.

In the far-off theaters of the war, the German African colonies had been taken by Franco-British native and white troops; that portion of the German dream had been eliminated. The Middle East was fast being won by the British, and the Kaiser's Berlin-to-Bagdad railroad remained only an unrealized vision.

General Erich von Falkenhayn, the German commander on the Western Front, evaluated the war situation without emotion; he balanced the good against the bad and came up with a realistic appraisal. His conclusion was that unless Germany won the war in the West as soon as possible, disaster loomed. He based this assumption on the cold fact that time was not on the side of Germany and her cohorts; if the war dragged

General Henri Philippe Petain (left), to whom the defense of Verdun was entrusted, gained the title "Saviour of France" for holding the stronghold against the Germans. Handsome General Erich von Falkenhayn (right) conceived the strategy of forcing the French to hold a vital point until they had been "bled white."

on much longer, the blockade would strangle the Fatherland.

To forestall such an eventuality, von Falkenhayn proposed an offensive in the West; he believed Russia was finished, so maximum German forces could be mobilized by denuding the Eastern Front. Von Falkenhayn craftily planned to focus his attack against the French, choosing as his objective the fortress city of Verdun. The German commandant felt sure the French would fight there to the end, for the loss of Verdun would indicate that France admitted her defeat in the war.

"If we plan properly at Verdun," von Falkenhayn declared, "we can bleed the enemy white by forcing him to throw in more and more men, until he has given everything. . ."

German casualties would be kept to a minimum by utilizing the largest artillery concentration. Against Verdun, von Falkenhayn brought guns ranging from

Map of the Verdun area shows the extent of the fighting. Heavy lines indicate German advance from February 21, when the attack began, through May, 1916. Before year's end, the French won back all the ground they had lost.

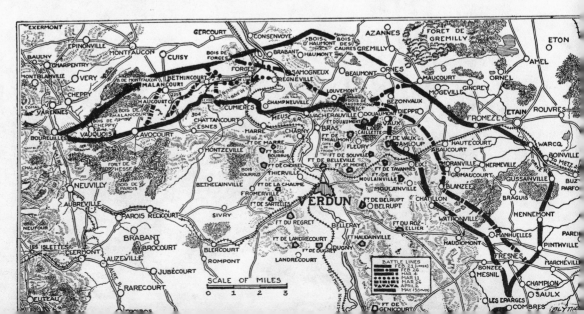

(Opposite page) *They marched into battle filled with ardor for the Kaiser and the Fatherland, these dead German infantrymen lying in their trench atop a hill near Verdun called Le Mort Homme (The Dead Man).*

A battery of French 75's (left) batter the advancing Germans during a phase of the fighting around Verdun. Smashed vehicles, splintered trees and water-logged shell holes (below) are the aftermath of a German barrage on a road near Verdun.

field pieces to 12-inch naval rifles and 420 mm siege mortars. Such guns were capable of reducing most fortresses; they had worked at Liége, Namur, Maubeuge, and in the east. In view of the fate suffered by permanent fortifications, Pappa Joffre, in 1915, abandoned the Verdun forts and relied instead on a system of trenches to defend the sector.

Again Joffre's judgment had been faulty. The Verdun forts were far better constructed than either the Belgian or the Russian ones; more modern, they could resist the heaviest calibre shell. An army attacking the bastions of Verdun would have been slaughtered by the defending forces. All this, Joffre gave up for the dubious security of trenches.

Since 1914, there had been little fighting around Verdun; as a result, that front was held by second-rate troops, and some of the field fortifications had been neglected. Pappa Joffre refused to heed the repeated warning by Army Intelligence that the Germans were building up for an attack on Verdun.

Aerial reconnaissance photos showed huge ammunition dumps for the hundreds of guns the Germans had hauled up to pound Verdun. However, early in February, even Joffre admitted something could be afoot and reinforced Verdun with two crack divisions although still dubious about the real significance of the German activity there. "I do not believe Verdun to be the *boche* objective," Joffre declared, "else why would he be so obvious about his intentions?"

The Germans were obvious only because preparations on such a massive scale could not be concealed. On February 21, Joffre and all France learned von Falkenhayn's intentions. At dawn, that gloomy winter's day, German artillery opened a bombardment of incredible intensity. More than 2,000,000 shells pulverized the French positions.

When the barrage lifted, the Germans went "over the top." The colonel commanding one assault regi-

Fort Douaumont, one of Verdun's main bastions, as it appeared at the height of the struggle. Note steel pill box (right) and soldier standing in a shell hole (foreground).

A German (above) lies where he fell during a futile attack against a French position near Verdun. Thousands of the Kaiser's best troops found a grave instead of glory at Verdun. Remnants of a French infantry platoon (below) return to friendly lines after taking a German strongpoint. This assault party has been relieved by fresh troops and the weary men can take a brief rest before going back into battle.

ment assured his officers, "You will find nothing living out there; our artillery has killed every Frenchman."

The colonel was wrong. Somehow, the *poilus* (a nickname for the common soldier in the French Army) had survived the withering storm of high explosive. Although casualties had been heavy, enough men were left to man their machine guns. The over-confident Germans fell in windrows, but despite valiant resistance, the French were forced out of their first-line trenches.

Almost too late, Joffre ordered his troops back into the forts which they should have been occupying from the outset. They fought the Germans to a standstill from these strongpoints. Terrible battles raged for Verdun; never in any war had men died in such sickening numbers.

A new commander took charge of French fortunes at Verdun. General Henri Philippe Petain was placed in charge on February 25. The grim Petain revived the old slogan of the Marne—*"Ils ne passeront pas!"*—"They shall not pass!" This spirit prevailed although the Germans managed to capture Fort Douaumont and Fort Vaux, key points in the defensive network. (Fort Douaumont was so well constructed that when the French recaptured it in October, 1916, the interior was entirely undamaged although it had been pounded by 120,000 shells of the highest calibre.)

Such places as Dead Man's Hill and Hill No. 304 became famous; thousands upon thousands of Germans and Frenchmen sacrificed themselves at Verdun. It was madness to continue the battle, but neither side relented. Petain organized a motor truck supply line along a road known as *La Voie Sacrée*—the Sacred Way. Day and night, in all sorts of weather, the trucks rolled with rations, ammunition and reinforcements for Verdun.

The German attack continued until mid-July; then, in the mid-summer heat, the Kaiser's men could give no more. It was Petain's turn. He told his troops *"On les aura!"*—"We'll get them!"—and ordered an all-out assault. From August until the end of the year, the *poilus* pushed the enemy back; Fort Douaumont and Fort Vaux were retaken in skillful assaults. The back of the German threat was broken and General von Falkenhayn's theory proved fallible. Although the French had given 460,000 men to hold Verdun, the Germans had expended more than 300,000 troops in failing to take it.

The epic struggle at Verdun was considered a French victory, but the price in blood was a terribly high one. The French Army never quite recovered from that awful struggle, nor did the Germans ever regain full striking power after the ghastly fighting. Both sides had given their best. Verdun became for all time the symbol of man's fortitude and war's futility. . .

Escorted by a detail of guards, German prisoners taken at Verdun march off to prison camp (above).

As steel-helmeted French soldiers watch warily (above) from the shelter of a trench, Germans scamper across No Man's Land to surrender during the furious fighting that swirled around Fort Douaumont.

Men such as these poilus (below) halted the Germans at Verdun. Only the seriously wounded left the Verdun lines for hospitals. Slightly injured men remained at the front after treatment at a first aid station.

Tragedy on the Somme

In the long saga of English military history, the finest army ever raised by Great Britain was formed in 1915-1916. The War Minister, General Horatio Herbert Kitchener, had equipped and trained the new British Army which was composed of volunteers and conscripts (for the first time, England resorted to conscription).

The volunteers were the cream of British youth; students, athletes, sportsmen, actors, aristocrats and plain workers joined up and many thousands more were conscripted into the army.

Never had there been such a large and splendid British Army. German propagandists sneered at the mighty force and called it "Kitchener's Mob." "England . . . that nation of shopkeepers, can not produce

soldiers to equal ours . . ." a spokesman for the Kaiser reassured the German people.

Although German officials made contemptuous references about the British in public, there was grave concern that "Kitchener's Mob" would prove troublesome. The Kaiser's generals kept a wary eye on British moves in the West. It was anticipated that General Haig would strike along the Belgian coast where he could be assured of naval support.

But Haig and Joffre had other plans for the British Army; they chose to attack along the Somme River in a sector which the Germans had been fortifying for two years. Here the Kaiser's troops had burrowed thirty-foot-deep dugouts into the chalk hills, trenches were bolstered by concrete emplacements, and barbed wire entanglements ran forty and fifty yards wide. Pill boxes and bunkers dominated the terrain with their machine guns.

"A worse choice for an offensive action could not be imagined," wrote a military observer. "The defensive system ran in such depth that no army could break through. . ."

However, because the Somme was where the British and French army sectors linked up, Joffre in-

Strikingly martial in appearance Sir Douglas Haig (left) cuts a handsome figure astride his well-groomed charger. In a sector such as this (below, left), where the German defenses were strongest, Field Marshal Haig decided to attack on a 28-mile-wide front along the Somme River. It was to prove a tragic blunder for the British and their French allies. Marshall Joseph Joffre (below) concurred with Haig on mounting the pre-doomed Somme offensive.

Shell-hole (above) serves as an improvised gun position for these British artillerymen. Other craters act as caches holding shells to feed the gun. When the lines are reorganized, better gun sites will be prepared.

Artist's version of a high-explosive artillery bombardment (above, right) upon the German lines during a phase of the Somme Battle. Note artillery observers and telephone operator in the foreground.

Second wave of British infantry (right) goes "Over the Top" during Somme fighting. Litter bearer (center) accompanies attacking troops. Men of first wave can be seen far to the right as shells burst about them.

sisted on attacking there; Haig raised some objections but finally agreed. Elaborate preparations were made including a week-long barrage of high explosive shells; according to experts, a bombardment of that duration should "pound the enemy into submission. . ."

On July 1, 1916, at 7:30 A.M., fourteen British divisions, bolstered by five French divisions, jumped off on a 28-mile-wide front. The attackers were met by blistering machine gun fire; the artillery had neither silenced the Germans, nor even destroyed the barbed wire entanglements. On that awful day, the British lost more than 60,000 men. It was the blackest period the British Army had ever known.

Despite the terrible slaughter, Haig kept pressing for five months; for all the sacrifice, the British could gain only five miles. But during the course of the drawn-out battle, the British gave the world a glimpse of future warfare by introducing the tank on September 15. It was a premature preview; only 49 tanks waddled clumsily into the fray. They were too few, the operators too inexperienced, and the tactics too raw for any major gains to be made.

Just as the Germans had erred by using poison gas too soon, the British blundered with their tanks. However, those few tanks that eventually joined the battle proved effective. The Germans fled before the ungainly monsters that came on with bullets spitting from their machine guns, defying German counter-fire.

The tank was a brainchild of General Ernest Dunlop Swinton, British Royal Engineering Corps; but its development came about as the result of help from Winston Churchill to whom Swinton originally had shown his plans. The name tank was affixed to the new weapon only as a means of concealing its purpose until the first ones were revealed to the enemy on September 15.

By mid-October, heavy autumnal rains made a quagmire of the Somme battlefield. Men floundered in the morass. Horses, vehicles and guns sunk in the mud; trenches crumbled and shell holes filled with water. An eye witness described the Somme sector as: ". . . a wasteland pockmarked with ditches and holes; a desolate region of truncated trees and wrecked villages; every breeze was tainted by death. . ."

51

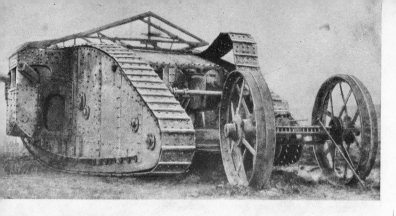

In September, 1916, the British uncovered a startling new weapon—the "tank." Properly employed it could have won the war for the Allies in 1916. German soldiers (below) swarm over stalled British tank in futile effort to destroy it.

It became impossible by November to carry on any further military operations. The Battle of the Somme came to a conclusion. That magnificent army, Kitchener's Mob, had been decimated—410,000 casualties. The French added another 200,000 men in killed, wounded, captured and missing. The Somme had reaped a crimson harvest. The scythe slashed deeply into German ranks, too. Over 500,000 soldiers became casualties for the Kaiser. That year, 1916, the Allies counted 1,200,000 total casualties on the Western Front while the Germans added a melancholy roster of 800,000 killed or maimed. The world was drowning in the blood of humanity and no man could foresee an end to the holocaust.

The monstrous holocausts of Verdun and the Somme had repercussions in both the German and the Allied armies. Pappa Joffre was promoted to the rank of Field Marshal and sent into retirement. His time of glory was over; it had ended at the Marne when Joffre's *poilus* threw back the German bid to end the war in 1914. He bade farewell to his soldiers and left the stage of history.

His successor was General Robert Georges Nivelle, young, dynamic and promising. Nivelle confidently assured the French that he would deal with the *boches*.

"You can look forward to a glorious victory in the Springtime," Nivelle vowed.

General von Falkenhayn, like Joffre, also fell from favor as a result of Verdun and the Somme. In August, 1916, he was relieved as chief-of-staff and replaced by Paul von Hindenburg and Erich von Ludendorff, the triumphant pair who had won such stupendous victories over the Russians.

Both the Allies and the Germans looked toward 1917 as the year of destiny; both predicted ultimate destruction of the enemy in the coming fateful year. . .

Russia's Glorious Hour

The Brusilov Offensive

Despite the shattering defeats of the previous year, the Czar's Army still retained its fighting spirit at the start of 1916. Manpower losses were quickly made up by recruits. The shortages of weapons and supplies grew less severe as British ships hauled material to Murmansk where it was trans-shipped along the newly completed Murmansk-Petrograd railway to the fighting fronts.

More supplies from England and France arrived at Vladivostok and were then loaded onto freight cars for the long journey to the capital via the Trans-Siberian railway. Despite great distances and bitter Russian winter, the equipment reached the troops. French and British officers came to train Russian soldiers and by spring a brand new Russian army stood ready for battle. Never before in the war had such splendidly outfitted and disciplined Russian divisions been prepared to take the field. The social evils that had been plaguing the country—the hunger, ignorance, incompetence and corruption—still festered. Rasputin held sway in the court; self-seeking men came to curry his favor. They bribed the avaricious Monk with money and jewels and he, in turn, won high positions for his "friends."

Patriotic Russians, young noblemen and many army officers, looked upon Rasputin with loathing. Some swore to break his hold on Czar Nicholas; but before they could take any steps the Eastern Front, which had been dormant for many months, suddenly exploded in dramatic activity.

The Germans had transferred thousands of troops to France during the battles of Verdun and the Somme, considerably weakening their forces opposing the Czarist armies. In the same period, the Austrians stripped the Russian Front of their most reliable troops for an offensive in Italy.

The Austro-Hungarian units left in Russia consisted of Czechs and other minorities, mainly Slavs who were only awaiting a chance to decamp. They were given this opportunity when without warning, on June 4, 1916, a huge Russian Army led by General Aleksey Brusilov opened an offensive on the Galician Front. This grand onslaught, which military historians named

A brilliant cavalry officer, General Aleksey Brusilov, led a great offensive against the Austrians on the Galician Front. His drive, which opened June 4, 1916, shattered Emperor Franz Josef's armies and sent them reeling back in retreat.

(Below) Newly equipped Russian troops respond with rousing cheers and raised bayonets to announcement that they would soon be at grips with the enemy. Both Germans and Austrians were astounded by the morale and spirit of Russian army after its shattering defeats in 1915.

Courageously pressing forward, the Russians fought like inspired men. They were unbeatable in the opening phases of Brusilov's great onslaught (above).

Terrified Austrians (below) throw up their hands in surrender as wild Cossack cavalrymen swarm down upon them. Note that Cossacks are armed with lance, saber and carbine. Few troops could withstand the full fury of a Cossack charge.

the Brusilov Offensive, struck with the force of an avalanche—everything was swept before the mighty Russian "steamroller."

Austro-Hungarian troops surrendered or deserted by the thousands; the Czechs came over carrying weapons and offering to fight against their Austrian oppressors.

"The death rattle is sounding in the throat of Franz Josef's Empire," wrote a contemporary journalist. "One great push and the whole rotten set-up will cave in."

Tremendous gaps yawned in the Austrian line and Russian columns poured through. Unfortunately for Brusilov, many regiments which he could have used as reserves had been wasted attacking Germans entrenched in the Pripet Marshes; as a result, Brusilov could not exploit his break-through to the fullest.

Meanwhile, the Austrians, appalled by Brusilov's success, cancelled their Italian offensive and sped reinforcements to stop the Russians. German troops were also thrown into the breach and by August, Brusilov's forward movement had halted.

At this time, Rumania joined the war on the side of the Allies. She had long awaited the right moment to strike at Austria; but Rumania dallied too long. Had she marched when Brusilov's push was advancing at full speed, the Rumanian Army could have swept into Austria virtually without opposition. But Rumanian politicians, greedy for huge territorial loot, bargained too long with Allied negotiators over the extent of Rumanian booty when Austria crumbled.

By the time their price was finally met, Brusilov had been stopped. German troops bolstered Bulgars, Turks and Austrians to snuff out Rumania less than four months after her entry into the war. The Rumanians lost more than half of their 500,000-man army in the debacle. Some Rumanian troops made a common front with the Russians along the Sereth River; but that too was overrun in still greater catastrophes to come.

Meanwhile, Brusilov tried in vain to keep his attack going, but the odds against him were too great. Not only did he have to fight the Germans and Austrians, but also the jealous generals on his own side—petty men who resented Brusilov's ascendency and

sabotaged his efforts. Supplies earmarked for the offensive were side-tracked. Brusilov's brave men marched without shoes, while cases of footgear lay stored in distant warehouses; his soldiers went hungry as piles of bacon rotted and sacks of flour became wormy in forgotten railroad sidings.

Even worse, Brusilov's artillery had no shells at hand when ammunition was plentiful. The envious bureaucrats preferred Brusilov's downfall to national victory. The grand offensive drowned in its own blood. More than 1,000,000 Russian soldiers were dead, wounded, captured or missing. Of the Germans and Austrians 600,000 became casualties and 400,000 were taken prisoner. The failure of the Brusilov Offensive

At the command "Forward!", Brusilov's men (above) sally out of their trenches in a headlong rush at the enemy. From June to August, 1916, the Russian offensive made tremendous gains, but by mid-August, German reinforcements had slowed Brusilov despite the bravery and self-sacrifice of his troops.

At last, heightened enemy resistance at the front and incompetence, bungling and petty jealousies in high places brought Brusilov to a standstill. His best soldiers died still valiantly attacking the foe. Note dead man caught on barbed wire clutching his rifle. More than 1,000,000 Russian casualties resulted from the Brusilov offensive.

finally broke the morale of the Russian soldier who now realized that the faith he had put in the Czar was misplaced.

The "Little Father" had led his children along the road of destruction. Those who had willingly, even gladly, spilled blood for the despot demanded revenge for all they had suffered. A slow-burning fire of revolution began spreading across the land.

In December, 1916, some misguided noblemen tried to solve all of Russia's problems by murdering Rasputin; they blamed the evil Monk for the nation's difficulties and felt that, if freed from his baleful influence, the Czar would lead the country to new glory. But the death of the charlatan had no effect upon Russia's destinies. Rasputin was merely a symptom and not a cause. Whispers of discontent rose to a shout, and still the Czar and his cohorts paid no heed to the ominous uproar among the masses.

That December, the Austro-Hungarian Empire also felt the reverberations of a mighty earthquake. The old regime quivered on the brink of ruin; Emperor Franz Josef died that fateful month to be succeeded by his nephew Carl. The empire which Franz Josef had established in 1848 was moribund. Mercifully, the old man did not live to see it crumble into rubble.

Even as Brusilov was stopped, Rumania went to war against Austria and Germany. Her poorly armed, badly trained troops went into the conflict with comic-opera gaiety. Here a Rumanian regiment meanders toward the front behind a fiddler playing lively native airs.

Grim-visaged Field Marshal August von Mackensen, wearing the uniform of the crack Death's Head Hussars, soon taught the Rumanians that war and violins did not mix. Von Mackensen led the Austro-German forces in a lightning attack on Rumania which soon destroyed that nation's army, quickly ending her bid for glory.

THE NAVAL WAR

1914-1918

The course of the war at sea was soon shaped by the nature of the opposing forces. The British Navy, long the ruler of the oceans, was seriously challenged by the German fleet; for the first time since the days of Lord Nelson, the British had a worthy foe at sea.

The focus of maritime action fixed upon Germany and Great Britain, the major naval powers of Europe. France dominated the Mediterranean, completely overpowering the weak Austrian fleet; the Germans had superiority in the Baltic and Black Seas since the Russians could not cope with the Kaiser's ships. The issue was clearly between Great Britain and Germany. From the outset, the British sought to establish a blockade of Germany, while the Germans attempted a blockade of the British Isles.

It was the hope of England's strategists to throttle German war potential by means of the blockade. Admittedly, this would be a slow effective process. The Germans realized that Great Britain was far more dependent than were they on seaborne traffic for food and war supplies. A successful blockade of Britain would wreck the Allies and end the war. Naturally, the

The huge 15-inch guns of the mighty battleship, H.M.S. Queen Elizabeth, symbolize England's sea power. At the outbreak of World War I, Britain "ruled the waves."

Great Britain's ally, Russia, had a small and obsolescent fleet for service in the Black Sea. Ships such as the cruiser Bogatyr (below) provided the backbone of the Russian fleet.

Kaiser Wilhelm II (on the left) holds a serious conference with his naval heads Admiral Alfred von Tirpitz and Admiral von Holtzendorff aboard a vessel of the Imperial Navy. Wilhelm's ambition was to wrest control of the seas from the English.

Battleships of the German Navy make an impressive sight as they proceed in majestic file through the waters of the North Sea while on maneuvers. Ships such as these offered stern opposition to British naval superiority.

Although Italy's land forces met with frequent setbacks at the hands of the Austrians, her navy was eminently successful against Franz Josef's fleet. Fast Italian torpedo boats frequently harrassed the Austrians in the Adriatic. Artist's version depicts sinking of Austrian battleship Szent Istvan by Italian torpedo boat in one of war's most daring naval feats.

Germans planned an all-out attempt to humble England.

When the war began, the British Navy counted 21 dreadnoughts (battleships) and nine giant armored cruisers. The Germans had 13 dreadnoughts and only four comparable cruisers. Both sides, however, had many destroyers and light cruisers. The British Navy in ships alone outnumbered the Germans about two-to-one, but the Kaiser owned a grim weapon for war at sea.

From the turn of the century, the Germans had paid special attention to submarines and submarine tactics. The torpedo was deadly when properly employed and no navy studied the possibilities of submarine warfare more thoroughly than did the Germans. The U-Boats (submarines) were manned by hand-picked volunteers and daring captains; a fleet of underwater craft was ready for action when the war began.

At that time, the Germans had a number of ships at sea or in the Orient and for a while these vessels ranged the oceans and raided Allied shipping. One by one they were hunted down and sunk by the British who also suffered some losses.

The *Emden,* the German raider commanded by Count Felix von Luckner, sunk many Allied merchantmen during the summer and autumn of 1914. But at last, von Luckner and his bold crew were trapped off the Cocos Island by an Australian Cruiser, H.M.A.S. *Sydney.* The *Emden* was destroyed and with her demise, there were no more German ships at large on the oceans.

Fast German cruiser Emden, which raided the world's commerce lanes during the early part of the war, is shown sinking the French destroyer Mousquet in a brief action. The Mousquet came upon the Emden somewhere in the Indian Ocean. Her efforts to torpedo the German raider failed and the French ship went down.

French mine sweepers clearing a field which Germans placed to block the North Sea. Germany, held in the vise of the British naval blockade, resorted to every sort of retaliatory measure in her effort to break the maritime stranglehold around her ports.

British battleship firing a practice broadside presents an awe-inspiring sight as she looses a salvo from her 15-inchers. World War I marked the rise of big-gunned warships.

59

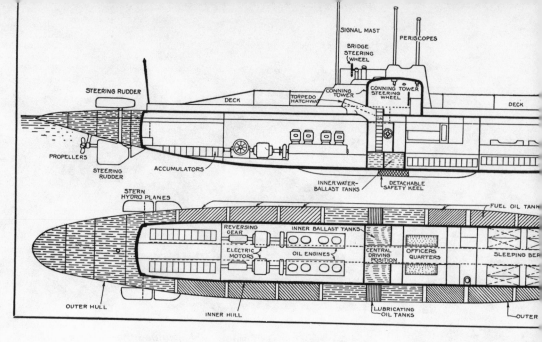

The U-Boats

Act I

(1914-1916)

The British blockade of Germany was carried out along rules that had been laid down many years earlier—long before submarines had been developed. The procedure was a cumbersome one—the blockading warship stopped a vessel suspected of carrying such contraband as arms or ammunition intended for a belligerent country. The merchantman was searched and then sent into port with a prize crew.

The British annoyed many neutrals by stopping their cargo ships, but no blood was spilled nor a single ship sent to the bottom.

The Germans, however, were unable to conduct such highly principled procedure; they had inferior surface forces and so could not stop vessels and search them for contraband. Either they had to abandon the idea of a counter-blockade or else employ unorthodox methods. They decided on the latter course.

Early in February, 1915, the German Admiralty proclaimed the waters around the British Isles a war zone and warned that all merchant shipping was subject to being sunk on sight by U-Boats which would constantly patrol the region although they had only 24 long-range submarines in operation and many gaps yawned in the U-Boat cordon.

It was not the first time the Germans had resorted to submarine warfare. On October 20, 1914, the U-17 made unpleasant history by sinking a freighter, the British merchantman *Glitra*, off the Norwegian coast. (On September 22, in the second month of the war, three British cruisers, the *Aboukir,* the *Cressy* and the *Hogue* fell victim to the torpedoes of a single submarine, the U-9.)

The German U-Boat war grew in frightfulness. Ships were sent to the bottom by lurking submarines in pitiless and relentless fashion. The British took steps to protect their merchant shipping; some vessels were armed, while submarine nets and mines were spread

As their answer to the British Blockade, the Germans resorted to unrestricted submarine warfare after February 1, 1915. All ships in waters adjacent to the British Isles were to be attacked by submarine commanders without warning. The U-Boat (submarine) was a complex vessel manned by highly skilled crews. Diagrammatic sketch (top) locates various sections of World War I U-Boat. Cross sectional drawing (above) shows works of U-Boat's deadliest weapon— the torpedo. Submarines also carried deck gun for use when the vessel surfaced, but depended mainly on torpedoes for sinking enemy ships.

Although submerged U-Boats could sneak up on a victim, the submarines did not always escape unscathed. This U-Boat, damaged by a British destroyer, was cast ashore on the French coast with the loss of all hands.

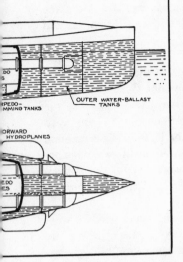

Artist Charles Pears captures a dramatic moment at sea (top) as a British sailing vessel, the H.M.S. Prize, sinks a surfaced U-Boat which thought the British vessel an easy prey.

Survivors of a torpedoed ship (above) are plucked out of the English Channel by patrol boats and other merchant vessels. Note man on life raft (foreground).

to protect shipping lanes. Fast motor-boats known as sub-chasers were developed. These speedy U-boat killers were equipped with special submarine detection devices, carried depth charges and other weapons especially designed for fighting the undersea craft.

Another method of counter-attack against U-Boats was a cleverly rigged decoy ship known as the Q-Boat. These were disguised so as to resemble harmless merchantmen, which offered tempting prey to the prowling submarines. The Q-Boat was loaded with timber and had guns concealed on her decks. When a sub torpedoed a Q-Boat, the cargo of timber kept her afloat; usually the U-Boat would surface and seek to finish off her victim with shell-fire from her deck gun. At this point the Q-Boat went into action. The masked batteries were revealed and the ship's guns would blast the submarine. Although the Q-Boat ruse was complicated, the system proved effective and disposed of at least a dozen U-Boats.

Actually, the best anti-submarine tactic was the convoy system; merchant ships sailed together in a stringent formation guarded by destroyers and other escort vessels. However, during the early years of the U-Boat campaign, convoys were not widely used. The mossbacks in the British Admiralty could not fully appreciate the need for them since shipping losses inflicted were not terribly high, due to a German shortage of submarines and crews to operate them rather than any Allied measures.

Among the numerous means employed by the Allies to combat the U-Boat menace was the so-called "Q" Boat. These were tramp steamers or freighters carrying concealed guns. A U-Boat captain, anxious to conserve his limited supply of torpedoes for more important targets, usually surfaced to finish off the old merchant ship. Once the submarine broke water, the "Q" Boat went into action with her rapid firing cannon.

GUN BEHIND BRIDGE SCREEN   GUN IN BOAT   GUN IN DECK-HOUSE

The Lusitania Incident

At 2:08 P.M., Friday, May 7, 1915, at a point some 10 miles off the Irish coast, the giant Cunard Line steamship, *Lusitania,* queen of Atlantic passenger ships, was torn by a rending explosion on her starboard side, just abaft the bridge.

The mighty liner, which carried 1,924 passengers, began to sink at the stern and listed sharply to starboard. Valiant efforts were made to lower lifeboats, but many aboard the doomed ship either went down with her or drowned after leaping overside. She took 1,198 men, women and children to the bottom. Of the 188 Americans on board, 114 met death on that sunny Friday afternoon in May.

A single torpedo from the German submarine U-20 had given the *Lusitania* her death blow. The instant the torpedo left its tube and churned through the calm waters to shatter the giant ship, war became inevitable between the United States and Germany. No single act previously committed by the Germans aroused such resentment in the United States as did the sinking of the *Lusitania.*

President Woodrow Wilson, who had declared American neutrality at the start of the European war, wrote a bitter note to the Imperial German Government protesting the sinking. Many Americans felt the President had not been forceful enough. There were cries of vengeance throughout the land; many prominent Americans demanded a declaration of war against Germany to ". . . make the Kaiser pay for the Americans who died on the *Lusitania* . . .", in the words of one leading politician.

Wilson silenced his critics and squelched the warmongers by giving the Americans a slogan: "We are too proud to fight!" But at the same time he kept applying pressure on the German government with increasingly sharp notes.

Count Johann von Bernstorff, the German Ambassador to the United States, sought to mollify American public opinion. He reminded the people that before the *Lusitania* had sailed from New York, her passengers had been warned through notices printed in the daily press that all ships bound for Great Britain were in danger of being sunk.

However, an incredibly tactless member of von Bernstorff's staff succeeded only in further irking Americans by declaring, "Surely, no one can blame the fate of the *Lusitania's* passengers upon the Imperial German Government. Those travellers were aware that destruction by our submarines was inevitable. It is not our fault if such persons wish to commit suicide."

The Germans claimed a legal and moral right to sink the *Lusitania* by charging that the liner's hold was crammed with ammunition; thus, she was a bona-

With 1,257 (and 667 crew) aboard, the S.S. *Lusitania*, pride of the Cunard Line, sails from New York, May 1, 1915, on a regular run to Liverpool, England. The giant vessel which displaced 30,395 tons was 755 feet long and 88 feet wide, the largest and fastest ship afloat at the time.

fide target for a U-Boat. The ship's manifest was lost at sea, the owners hotly denied the German allegations and the contents of the ill-fated vessel's hold has remained a mystery to this day.

Those Americans who died on the *Lusitania* were not the only United States citizens to lose their lives through U-Boat action. More passenger ships were sunk; more Americans went to their deaths. Acrimonious notes flew back and forth between Washington and Berlin. Tempers grew shorter and even Wilson doubted that the United States could maintain much longer its "too proud to fight" attitude.

However, after nearly a year of diplomatic exchanges, the Germans promised, in 1916, to limit their submarine attacks exclusively to cargo vessels and warships. U-Boat commanders were ordered to conduct future warfare along humane lines and whenever possible allow crews of merchant ships an opportunity to launch lifeboats before sinking the vessel. Despite modified U-Boat activity, 192,000 tons of shipping was sunk monthly in 1916 as against 1915's total of 113,000 tons per month. (These figures included vessels of all nations caught in the submarine zone.)

The full fury of U-Boat terror—which the Germans called *schrecklichkeit*—was yet to come. No man dared even imagine the awful months ahead when a desperate Germany, fighting for its life, loosed a storm of frightfulness at sea never before equalled in all history. . .

By Friday, May 7, 1915, the Lusitania was off the coast of Ireland. At 2:08 P.M., she was struck by a torpedo fired from the German submarine U-20. Eighteen minutes later, the great ship went down. She took with her 1,198 passengers and crewmen.

The Lusitania's survivors struggle in the waters of the Irish sea. Overloaded life boats capsized and many persons drowned because the ship went down so quickly that boats could not be launched.

The Clash of Navies

Jutland, 1916

Although the British and German navies clashed several times early in the war, no decisive battle was fought. This drawing shows the torpedo boat H.M.S. Meteor launching a deadly missile at the German cruiser Blucher (right).

Although units of British and German ships had met in roaring battle, the awaited confrontation between the Royal Navy and the German High Seas Fleet did not take place until May 31, 1916, off Jutland, Denmark.

Earlier naval fighting had revealed that both fleets possessed good morale and fighting skill. Daring German maritime raids struck the English coast in December, 1914. The Kaiser's warships bombarded the towns of Whitby and Scarborough causing many civilian casualties.

One German sortie, aimed at destroying the British North Sea fishing fleet ended disastrously when a squadron of British battle cruisers under Rear Admiral David Beatty intercepted the raiders. In the brief engagement that followed, the German cruiser *Blücher* was sunk with a heavy loss of life.

Both sides suffered casualties in subsequent maritime battles, but not until Jutland did the naval warfare have any real significance. The Battle of Jutland began as a running fight between enemy cruisers; it ended in a wild melee of ships, guns and torpedoes. For a time, the German fleet under Admiral Rheinhold Scheer appeared hopelessly trapped by superior forces, but the British commander, Admiral John Jellicoe, fumbled his chance to crush the German Fleet and Scheer escaped. On paper, Jutland was a German victory: the British lost three battle cruisers, three armored cruisers and

Results of Meteor's torpedo are seen as the stricken Blucher turns over on her side and sinks. Note crew members clinging to the side of the careening vessel. Dramatic photograph was taken from a British warship participating in the action.

A critical moment in the Battle of Jutland is caught by artist Charles Pears as the German Grand Fleet hoves into sight on the horizon (background). British battle cruisers and their destroyers turn to meet the enemy. Water spouts from German shells spurt up around the ships of the Royal Navy.

A hard-hitting sea dog, Admiral Sir David Beatty (left), led the battle cruiser squadron of the Royal Navy against the Germans in the crucial Battle of Jutland. A belated casualty was Lord Horatio Herbert Kitchener (center), Britain's War Minister. Admiral Sir John Jellicoe (right) seen in full dress uniform was commander-in-chief of the British Fleet.

In a furious swirl of naval action, a German cruiser, sheathed in flames, is bracketed by British shells and goes to her death with guns still blazing defiance in Battle of Jutland.

eight destroyers; the Germans had one battle cruiser, an old battleship, four light cruisers and five destroyers sunk. In men, British casualties numbered more than 6,000 killed, wounded and missing; German casualties stood at nearly 3,000.

The "victorious" German Navy, nevertheless, fled ignominiously from the field; although battered and bleeding, the British Lion still remained supreme. Once back at its bases, the German Fleet did not emerge to fight another surface engagement for the rest of the war.

Thus Jutland, the war's biggest naval battle, was turned into a British triumph by default. Admiral Jellicoe's conduct of the fight was scarcely in the highest traditions of the Royal Navy; he was somewhat less than Nelsonian. Had Jellicoe shown the dash and brashness of his naval forebears, Scheer's ships would have lined the bottom of the North Sea that fateful May day.

The clash off Jutland had a long-range effect on the war at sea. Inaction gradually sapped the morale of the German Navy; sedition, mutiny and insurrection finally corroded the fleet. The unrealistic German fear

of another surface battle gave additional importance to the submarine as an offensive naval weapon. It was this reliance on U-Boats combined with other factors which eventually brought the United States into the war as a combatant against Germany.

Jutland had another after effect. The Germans had sown mines around the Orkney Islands prior to the battle. In June, 1916, Lord Kitchener, England's Minister of War, was sailing to Russia aboard the fast cruiser *Hampshire*. The vessel struck a German mine off the Orkneys and went down with nearly all hands in a raging storm. So died Horatio Herbert Kitchener, one of Britain's most revered military figures. He had won his glory years before during the fighting in Egypt and the Sudan; Kitchener was not a 20th-century soldier. His day was in the past when the British square was unbeatable and hard-riding cavalry pressed home the charge with saber and carbine.

Although he had muddled many times in World War I, Kitchener left behind him a remarkable monument—the new British armies he raised and trained, the stubborn divisions of conscripts affectionately called "Kitchener's Mob."

By 1917, when Germany returned to a policy of unbridled submarine warfare, she possessed many newly built U-Boats equipped with wireless and better armed than those of the 1914-1916 period. The U-36 shown here (top, opposite page) on trial spin was typical of modern undersea killers spreading havoc on world's shipping lanes.

Passengers and crew members of torpedoed liner (right) crowd a hastily lowered lifeboat. This shot was taken from the deck of the sinking ship.

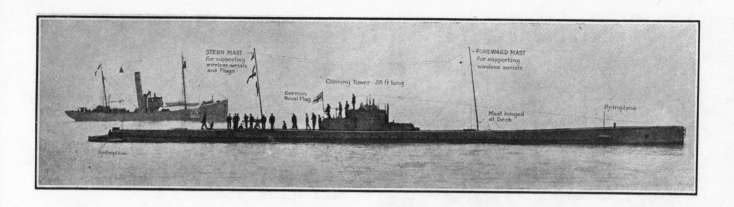

The U-Boats, Act II (1917-1918)

The U-Boats did not have things all their own way. In this illustration, a Royal navy destroyer, summoned by a radio call from a hovering British dirigible, despatches a German submarine with a well-aimed shot from her forward cannon.

The U-Boats were countered with convoys of merchantmen escorted by destroyers and long-range aircraft which brought hundreds of ships carrying war cargoes safely into British and French ports.

By February 1, 1917, the Germans had 120 U-Boats capable of long-range missions at sea. Many were of the most modern type, equipped with the latest torpedoes and other armament.

A knotty decision faced German planners in 1917. The Allied blockade was seriously affecting the home front. Shortages of all kinds plagued Germany. The war was at a stalemate on all fronts and no end seemed to be in sight. In despair, the Germans ordered a renewal of unrestricted submarine warfare. "Sink on sight!" U-Boat captains were ordered. No ship was to be spared regardless of nationality or cargo.

"We took this step knowing that it might cause the intervention of the United States against us," recalled a German official. "It was believed by our policy makers that even if the Americans went to war, our U-Boats would starve Great Britain into surrender within six months, long before America could arm and train any sizeable forces."

The best minds of Germany guessed wrong. The second U-Boat campaign proved a fatal error for Germany although at its outset it seemed to be a complete success. The score of ships sunk by submarines soared phenomenally: 236 ships went down in February, 338 in March, 430 in April.

Food stocks in Britain fell to a six weeks' supply after April. Those who knew the situation dolefully predicted that Great Britain must surrender by November, 1917, unless a dramatic change took place.

German submariners cluster about deck gun of U-Boat as surfaced craft plows through choppy Atlantic.

Anti-submarine mines took a toll of U-Boats. An Italian minelayer drops lethal load at designated points in Mediterranean while travelling at full speed.

English tars pick up rescued German sailor who waves encouragement to comrade swimming toward the British sub.

Much credit for the efficiency
with which the U.S. Navy went into combat was given
the energetic Assistant Secretary of the Navy,
Franklin Delano Roosevelt.

Irish fishermen (left, foreground) hail flotilla of
U. S. destroyers speeding toward England.
Waterspout marks point where shell from
subchaser's bow gun has scored on U-Boat (below).

That summer, the convoy system was adopted. Units of the U. S. Navy helped shepherd merchant ships after the United States had declared war on Germany in April. Escort vessels equipped with submarine detection devices and improved depth charges made it dangerous to attack convoys. So many submarines were destroyed by surface vessels that in October, 1917, only 215 merchantmen went down as a result of U-Boat action as compared to 430 in April. So effective were the convoys that only one ship out of every 200 was lost to submarines.

The U-Boats were hit hard by Anglo-American minefields laid in 1917-1918. During the early part of 1918, the British made two daring raids, one aimed at Ostend and the other at Zeebrugge, two important

Belgian ports used as submarine bases. The attack on Ostend was repulsed, but the Zeebrugge foray attained success; the British sunk three old ships across the harbor mouth and blocked the exit so that the U-Boats based on Zeebrugge were penned up for the duration of the war.

By mid-1918, the tonnage of ship construction exceeded the amount destroyed by submarines. The campaign of terror at sea failed in 1914-1918 during World War I as it did in 1939-1945 when the Second World War raged. The *schrecklichkeit* by which the Germans sought to break the spirit of the Allies was twice unsuccessful. Neither the Kaiser nor Hitler correctly assessed the will and courage of free men who resisted tyranny with their hearts, strength and lives. . .

THE WAR IN THE SKY   1914-1918

Aircraft moved ahead with giant strides during the First World War. The primitive craft of 1914, such as the Valkyrie Monoplane (top, left), were toys when compared with the Spad fighters (right) and Sopwith Camel (top, right) of 1917-1918, although by modern standards even the best planes of World War I are museum pieces. Note bird-shaped German aircraft of type known as "Taube" being hotly pursued by unwieldy French-built plane early in the war (below, left).

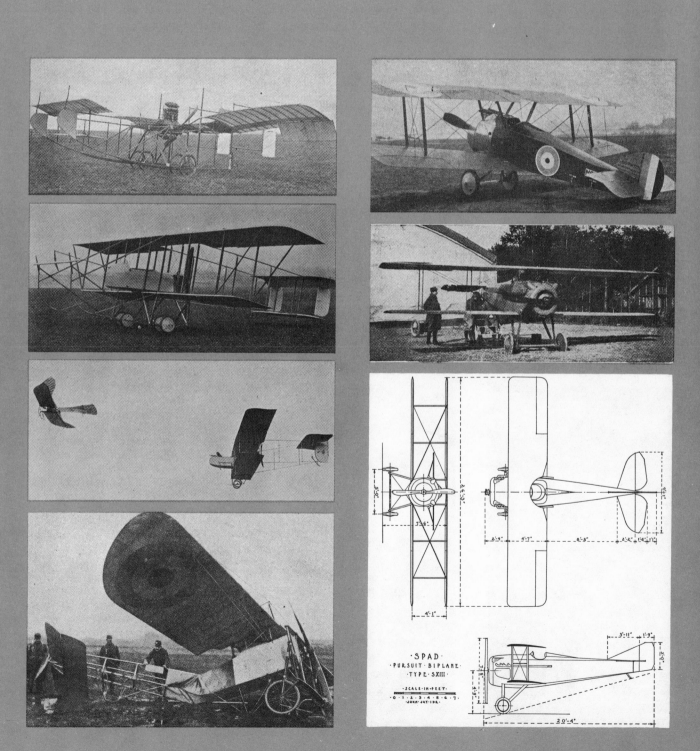

When the Great War started in August, 1914, airplanes had never before been used in warfare. Although Orville and Wilbur Wright had flown the first power-driven airplane only eleven years earlier, hydrogen-filled rigid airships as well as seaplanes and landplanes were in the military service of most countries by 1914.

The airships could maintain sustained flight and carry substantial weights, but the planes were frail, flimsy machines made of wood, wire and canvas. Most were "pusher" type biplanes with the engine in the rear, able to do about 70 m.p.h. at a height of two miles. These primitive craft were able to stay aloft only about three hours. Seaplanes, equipped with floats, were carried on some naval ships; they were lowered into the water and raised from it by means of a special hoisting device.

At the outset of the war, airplanes were considered to be suitable solely for reconnaissance. They proved so effective that both sides developed fighter aircraft designed to shoot down enemy reconnaissance planes. By early 1915 the "pusher" was obsolete. The latest planes had front engines and propellers. They were fast and maneuverable, but finding ways for the pilot to fire his machine gun at an enemy aircraft presented a problem.

A flier with a machine gun mounted in the cockpit, firing straight ahead, was liable to shoot off his own propeller. Yet, this was the most logical place for the weapon. The Germans solved the difficulty in 1915. Their speedy Fokker monoplanes were fitted with a synchronizing device which prevented the gun from firing when the propeller blade passed directly in front of the muzzle. For a time, this gave the Germans

superiority in the air, but soon enough both the British and French had similar equipment.

The war in the sky was improvised from the beginning. No manuals existed for air war and combat tactics had to be originated. Daring fliers such as the Germans: Max Immelmann and Baron Manfred von Richthofen; the Frenchmen: Charles Nungesser, René Fonck and Georges Guynemer; and the Englishmen: Albert Ball and Billy Bishop, created a new type of warfare. They engaged in maneuvers which defied all rules of flying, but created the pattern for all future fighter and bomber pilots. As airplanes came into common usage, individual "dog-fights" were replaced by mass battles with hundreds of planes participating.

The Germans had long considered the feasibility of attacking by air enemy factories and cities far behind

The rigid, gas-filled, motor-driven airship called the Zeppelin, after its inventor Count Ferdinand von Zeppelin, was Germany's prime terror weapon at the beginning of the war bombing such centers as London and Paris.

The Zeppelins were themselves highly vulnerable to attack since gas bags were inflated with inflammable hydrogen. Allied fliers soon made a sport of what they called "Zep Busting" (left).

Planes were used from war's outset not for fighting purposes but flew reconnaissance missions and also dropped propaganda over enemy troops. Here (far, left) French plane distributes leaflets to Germans below reassuring potential deserters that captured men are well fed and looked after.

Once air fighting tactics had been originated, duels in the sky between enemy fliers grew commonplace. Drawing shows two British Sopwith Camels tangling with superior force of German planes in a wild, dog fight somewhere over the Western Front.

Among outstanding heroes of aerial warfare was Baron Manfred von Richtofen, known as "Germany's Red Knight." This brilliant flier accounted for 80 enemy planes before he was downed in 1918.

As the war continued the Germans designed huge bombing planes such as this Gotha, a twin-engined craft carrying three men, two gunners and a pilot, for long-range bombing runs, usually aimed at cities.

the frontlines. However, in 1914, there were no planes capable of carrying a sufficient bomb load for this purpose.

The big Zeppelin airship was constructed especially for bombing the foe's industrial centers and large cities. The "Zeps" had a longer range and could attain greater heights than any plane extant at the time. Zeppelins made more than 200 attacks upon Britain, including 51 on London. Though damage and casualties were small by present standards, the raids created great alarm among civilians. The era of total war was on its way. (Paris and other French cities also suffered Zeppelin raids and later in the war, when the Germans had a huge bomber known as the *Gotha,* Paris frequently was subjected to aerial bombardment.)

The Zeppelin menace ended when there appeared fighter planes of enough speed and climb to overtake the huge ships. A few bursts from a Lewis machine gun sent the lumbering "Zep" plunging to earth in flames. Also, as efficient anti-aircraft guns developed, the Zeppelins became easy targets for hawkeyed gun-

Captain Georges Guynemer, killed in a dog fight over Belgium on September 11, 1917, shot down 53 German planes. French air ace Rene Fonck was second only to von Richtofen as war's top pilot, with 75 victories.

These neatly aligned German planes are part of famous squadron which von Richtofen commanded. His "Flying Circus" was manned by the best pilots in the German Air Force. Hermann Goering, who gained infamy under Adolf Hitler, flew with von Richtofen's "Flying Circus." While dog fight rages between British and Germans, Canadian pilot, Roy Brown, pours a stream of lead into Baron von Richtofen's triple-winged red Fokker. As depicted by artist, German ace slumps over dead at the controls of his speedy triplane.

As German ship plunges out of control, observer is thrown out, and Guynemer speeds by having chalked up his forty-fifth kill.

ners. By 1916, the big airships were no longer used for bombing missions. They remained in service, however, as reconnaissance craft for the German Navy and did effective work in that capacity.

During the last year of the war, 1918, the airplane came into its own as a military weapon. Combat aircraft with speeds of 160 m.p.h. and ceilings of 20,000 feet flew daily.

In 1918, heavy British bombers (the De Havilland for day attacks and the Handley Page for night work) were dropping 500 tons of bombs on German industrial centers, railroads, bridges and other military targets. And it was in 1918 that the first aircraft carrier successfully launched fighter planes. On July 19, 1918, the British launched seven Sopwith Camels from the deck of the carrier *Furious*.

Aviation played an increasingly active role in the ground fighting during 1918. Even the most conservative staff officer had to concede that victory on the ground depended on supremacy in the air. The tiny air forces of 1914 grew to tremendous size four years later. In 1918, the British had 2,600 aircraft in operation; the French, 3,857; the Germans, 2,800; the Italians, about 800. The U. S. Army Air Service numbered 740 planes, Austria had nearly 600 and the Belgians, 150.

The best Allied craft were the British DH4, the Sopwith Camel, the Bristol, the Handley Page, the Italian Caproni, the French Spad, Nieuport and Bréguet. The Germans had the Albatross single seater, Fokker monoplanes, biplanes and triplanes and the Pfalz.

There were heroes in every air force, immortals of aerial combat. The most outstanding Americans were the survivors of the famed Lafayette Escadrille who had volunteered to fight for France in 1916—men such as Raoul Lufberry, Frank Luke, and many others. But the Yanks had other great fliers who had not been with the Escadrille: foremost was Eddie Rickenbacker who commanded the 94th Aero Pursuit Squadron in France. He won the Congressional Medal of Honor for shooting down 25 Germans.

Not only the men, but the machines and the tactics as well were the pioneers of military aviation. The airplane became a crude instrument of destruction in the First World War; by 1939, when the Second World War began, it was no longer a primitive weapon. Yet, all functions of aircraft during World War II originated in 1914-1918—reconnaissance, bombardment, artillery spotting, troop strafing, tactical and strategical bombing, the aircraft carrier and torpedo bombing.

The First World War transformed flying from a curiosity to a commonplace activity. The birth of modern commercial aviation stemmed directly from the wire, wood and canvas "kites" flown by reckless young men nearly a half-century ago.

Captain Eddie Rickenbacker (center, above, left) chalked up 26 German planes to be America's top ace and win the Congressional Medal of Honor. Captain William Bishop (above) was Canada's greatest war hero. His score of 72 German aircraft shot down won him the Victoria Cross.

These Americans gave their lives fighting for France as members of the Lafayette Escadrille. Shown here are; Sergeant-Pilot Victor Chapman, Raoul Lufberry playing with the Escadrille's lion cub mascots, Sergeant-Pilot Norman Prince and (below, left and right) Sergeant-Pilot Kiffin Rockwell and Sergeant-Pilot James Roger MacConnell. Two other members of the Lafayette Escadrille are Captain Robert Nordhoff and Captain James Hall, co-authors of Mutiny on the Bounty (center photo, below).

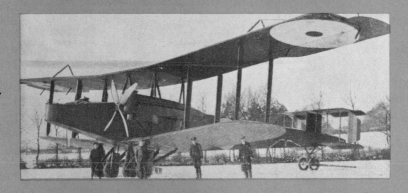

Planes in service at the end of the war showed vast improvements in design. The British Handley-Page Bomber (top, left) was spreading havoc over German-held territory, while the triplane Italian built Caproni (above, right) could carry a dozen passengers plus a bomb-load. The Nieuport fighter (top, right) could rise 7,000 feet in six minutes and had a ceiling of 20,000 feet. The Breguet Bomber (at left) was capable of hauling heavy bomb loads over great distances.

In 1914, before bombing techniques were improved, both sides used to drop high explosives on the enemy in this primitive fashion. Before the war was over, however, big bombing planes were flying in huge formations on their missions of destruction. Artist depicts Allied aircraft blasting German bases in Belgium (right).

In the closing weeks of the war, the Allied air arm saw much action. A squadron of Spads (below) is seen supporting tank-led French infantry pursuing fleeing Germans at right. With machine guns spitting, Spads rake retreating enemy.

German infantrymen fight back against strafing British planes (left). British plane (center) parachutes ammunition to forward machine gunners whose lines of supply have been cut by German artillery fire. Magazine illustrator Joseph Simpson imaginatively portrays a night bombardment by an R.A.F. plane at moment that exploding missiles blast a train (right) as aircraft's gunner sprays the railroad cars with machine gun bullets.

THE MOMENTOUS YEAR 1917

Western Front

"I promise you that we shall clear the *boches* from our sacred soil before 1917 passes into history," declared General Robert Georges Nivelle, who had replaced Pappa Joffre.

Nivelle was more bombast than prudence. He bragged that his offensive would crack the German lines "as a mallet shatters a walnut." Totally disregarding the disastrous frontal offensives of 1914, Nivelle ignored all advice and continued to loudly plan his campaign. Seldom was a military secret more poorly kept. Nivelle announced his intentions to all within earshot; consequently, the Germans knew as much about them as did Nivelle's staff officers.

Instead of waiting for the talkative Frenchman to strike, the Germans moved first under General Erich von Ludendorff's brilliant guidance. That wily general upset Nivelle's calculations by retreating from the very area at which the French attack was aimed, the so-called Noyon Bulge.

Von Ludendorff retired to a series of prepared and well fortified positions known as the Hindenburg Line. In some sectors the Germans fell back to a distance of thirty-one miles. Von Ludendorff ordered his troops to apply the "scorched earth" policy in the salient they abandoned. The Germans left a swath of destruction behind them. Wells were poisoned; roads mined; houses burned.

"No grass grows, no birds sing, nothing is to be seen but charred ruins and shattered trees. The *boches* have made a wasteland of the countryside. . ." wrote a French correspondent who travelled over the region.

Nivelle watched undismayed as von Ludendorff foiled him. The braggart simply made new plans and again boasted that he would "crush" the enemy. German agents soon learned Nivelle intended to attack between Soissons and Rheims during April; von Ludendorff efficiently prepared a reception for the French.

However, it was the British who began the annual slaughter in the West with an attack at Arras, the northern anchor of the Hindenburg Line, which lasted from Easter morning, April 9, until April 24. Canadian troops gallantly stormed Vimy Ridge, the high ground that dominated the terrain. The offensive gained only five miles along a twenty-mile-wide front. Some 18,000 Germans and 230 guns were captured; about 57,000

Arrogant, pompous General Robert Nivelle replaced Pappa Joffre as commander-in-chief and bragged that he would drive the Germans from France in 1917. Instead of awaiting Nivelle's onslaught, the Germans under von Ludendorff and von Hindenburg pulled back to stronger positions. Dotted line running from Arras through St. Quentin indicates course of famous "Hindenburg Line," considered to be the most strongly fortified sector in the world.

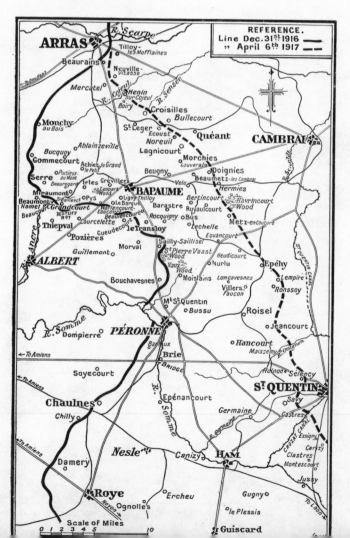

As Germans retreated they followed a "scorched earth" policy; wells were poisoned, crops burned, farm animals slain. This scene of devastation is an example of their handiwork.

Not Nivelle, but General Douglas Haig began the spring offensive by attacking the Germans around Arras, on Easter Sunday, April 9, 1917. Tommies file past field guns on way to the firing line.

Second wave of Canadian infantry scramble out of trenches in assault on vital Vimy Ridge which they finally took after great cost. Dimly seen in background are men of the first wave occupying an advanced trench.

Battle-wise British infantrymen dash through the rubble-littered streets of a French town during the Battle of Arras. German shells are exploding in the background and the troops are racing to take cover.

additional casualties were inflicted upon the enemy, but the insignificant advance cost the British 84,000 men.

On April 16, a week after the British attack opened, Nivelle ordered an 11,000,000 shell bombardment to herald the opening of his offensive along a fifty-mile front from Soissons to Rheims. Known as the Second Battle of the Aisne, Nivelle's grand attack petered out in its first day although the swaggering general kept driving his men to slaughter until late May. By then the French had lost 120,000 men and a serious mutiny broke out in the French Army; whole divisions refused to go back into the front lines. Some units raised the red flag and France seemed on the verge of revolution.

Nivelle was sacked and his place taken by General Henri Philippe Petain, the "Saviour of Verdun." He had a difficult task; because of the mass mutiny, the French front was held by relatively few troops. If the Germans learned what was happening, they could easily have broken through to victory.

Petain once again saved his country. He visited the

mutinous units, satisfied the men's grievances and gradually restored morale. Some leaders of the mutineers were courtmartialled and executed; several troublesome outfits were annihilated by shellfire from loyal batteries, but the main mutiny was suppressed without bloodshed because the *poilus* trusted Petain and believed in him.

By late July, the danger of a revolution had passed. Oddly, even at the height of the disaffection, the Germans had no inkling that the French Army was almost impotent. As one mutineer put it, "This was a family quarrel. We wanted no one else to know; least of all the *boches*. Even though we hated Nivelle and all he represented, we hated the *boches* far more. . ."

At any rate, the Germans lost a fine chance to end the war triumphantly in the West. For the remainder of the year, Petain kept the French army on the defensive, although he did launch two successful limited attacks near Verdun and on the Chemin des Dames, a 650 foot high eminence. But throughout 1917, the burden of fighting on the Western Front passed from French hands to the British.

Cautious Tommies explore captured enemy trench, bayonets ready to deal with German resistance from a dug-out. Nivelle's attack along a fifty-mile front between Soissons and Rheims was preceded by an 11,000,000 shell barrage. Numberless shell casings fired by batteries of 75's lie at the side of a road (below, right).

(Opposite page) Despite the intense barrage, Nivelle's onslaught, known as the Second Battle of the Aisne, brought slaughter instead of victory to the French. More than 120,000 poilus fell in the terrible fighting. At some points, the French scored local triumphs such as these surrendering Germans (left, center).

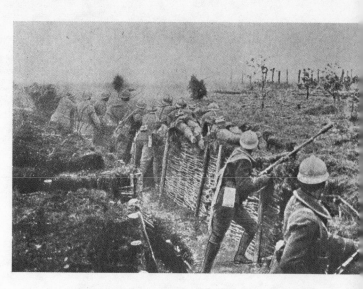

Efficient German gun crew blasts away at advancing French with great effect. German artillery was handled with uncanny accuracy, attesting to training and discipline of the Kaiser's soldiers.

French shock troops prepare for a charge as picked rifle grenade men await signal to bombard enemy lines with a barrage of deadly missiles.

Battle-weary French infantry troops rest on a shell-torn ridge while the battle rages in front of them. Nivelle's grand offensive was a complete failure. It caused a widespread mutiny throughout the French army as the men tired of the senseless slaughter.

Mud, Blood and Death
The Third Battle of Ypres

During the summer of 1917, General Sir Douglas Haig undertook a British offensive in Flanders. This attack turned into the Third Battle of Ypres, one of the bloodiest and most desperate struggles of the war. Tommies are shown escorting German prisoners through shattered Ypres. Note captured men carrying litter. Ruined building in background is city's famous landmark, Cloth Hall.

General Sir Douglas Haig had long been planning an offensive in Flanders to recapture the Belgian Channel ports which would have been a rich prize. The Ypres salient was chosen as the battleground. Tommy Atkins, the prototype of the common British soldier, called the city "Wipers." He knew it only too well, having fought there since 1914.

Haig planned carefully and moved against Messines Ridge to the south of Ypres; for weeks, parties of British and German sappers had been honeycombing the Ridge with mines and countermines. But the British acted first. They detonated 500 tons of high explosives at 1:30 A.M., June 7, after a 17-day bombardment of the German positions. The mighty explosion turned the crest of the ridge into a man-made volcano. A swift assault by British infantry wrested Messines Ridge from the stunned defenders. Once the position was secure, Haig turned his attention to the Ypres salient.

All through July, the guns bombarded German positions. That month, the weather turned abnormally rainy and the Flanders soil became a vast bog. The once fertile land was transformed into "a sea of treacherous slime. . .", a journalist wrote.

The main British attack jumped off on July 31. It stalled in the mire almost immediately. Guns sank to their hub caps; horses and mules drowned; men wallowed in waist-deep mud. There was no possibility that Haig's offensive could gain the channel ports in that welter of mud but the British kept attacking, floundering in the mud and dying.

A new dimension was added to the horrors of the war when the Germans used "mustard gas" for the first time; this noxious chemical caused agonizing burns and blisters. The heroic Canadians captured Passchendale Ridge, a key point, in November, but the Third Battle of Ypres was an expensive failure; the British lost nearly 380,000 men as against 190,000

Heavy guns of the Royal Field Artillery kept up an incessant pounding of German lines. Shell holes filled with stagnant water during heavy rainfalls and turned Flanders into a vast bog. ➤

The Great Push—Bombers holding a point of vantage whilst Lewis guns are hurried up—the attack swarming up through Messines' ruins after the front trench system had been breached by the mine explosions

Eyewitness sketch catches furious action on crest of Messines Ridge, key point to Ypres salient. Tommies swarmed up ridge after British land mine had destroyed main German trench system. Fierce hand-to-hand fighting preceded British capture of vital position.

Third Battle of Ypres stalled in the mud and slime of Flanders. British tank sinks in marshy earth as continual rains turn entire region into a swampland.

dead, wounded, captured or missing Germans.

The only good news for the British occurred from November 20 - December 7, when a perfectly planned attack led by almost 400 tanks was launched at Cambrai. The ground in the sector chosen was well drained and solid. The tanks came of age in that battle; they waddled across No Man's Land, closely followed by infantry, to punch a four-mile-wide dent in the Hindenburg Line around Cambrai. Unfortunately, Haig did not have sufficient reserves in tanks or men to properly exploit the advantage. Nevertheless, Cambrai showed that tanks, correctly used, could break the stalemate of trench warfare.

The year closed in the West on a dour note for the Allies, yet 1917 also brought a great gleam of hope. Although a revolution in Russia had overthrown the Czar and removed Russia from the war, the United States was now in the lists against Germany. Soon, very soon, hordes of fresh American soldiers would be pouring into the lines to bolster the flagging British and French.

And France, which had been on the verge of disaster in 1917, now rose again in its stalwart strength with a man of furious energy and unshakeable courage as its new Premier—Georges Clemenceau. He fiercely hated the Germans and knew how to whip his countrymen to greater efforts and further sacrifice. Clemenceau was most appropriately known as "The Tiger."

Even the long-suffering army horses could not cope with Flanders-style mire. Living conditions on the Ypres front were intolerable for humans and animals alike.

Kilted Scottish troopers mount guard as wounded German prisoners receive treatment at a British aid station in a war-torn town. This photograph focusses in stark detail the grimness, dirt and squalor of war. Note bullet holes in wall of wrecked building.

Supply convoy heading for front during bloody
Battle of Passchendale is halted by German shell fire.
Shell is exploding to left of road in a near miss.

Fantastic pattern of devastation marks road
in France. Tree skeletons stand like ghostly sentries
alongside battered roadway. Allied soldier
peers cautiously from behind charred tree trunk to
identify approaching cars in distance.

Georges Clemenceau, known as "The Tiger
of France," was made premier of his country in
November, 1917. A relentless foe of the
Germans, Clemenceau was determined to crush
France's ancient enemy. At one time in his long
career, Clemenceau, a physician, practiced medicine
in New York City. His office was located at Seventh
Avenue and West Twelfth Street.

(Opposite) British troops from north of England
rest in Flanders shell holes while awaiting signal to
attack during Ypres fighting.

Rasputin was dead, but everything remained the same in Russia. All through the bitter winter of 1916-1917 starvation, disease and death stalked through Russia. In peasant shacks and workers' shanties, mourning candles burned for the young men who had fallen in Brusilov's Offensive. A shudder of revulsion against the Czar wracked the country. Discontent crept among the Dark People. The revolutionaries—the socialists and communists—emerged from their hiding places and began agitating for a change in government. Men and women risked imprisonment, exile, even execution passing out leaflets which urged the people to rise against the Czar.

In Petrograd street demonstrations, organized by the socialists and communists, took place. Crowds shouting for bread were brutally dispersed by mounted Cossacks. The masses who had once sung the Russian national anthem "Long Live the Czar!" now chanted the song of the revolution, "The Internationale" and its words rang out in the brittle winter air,

"Arise ye prisoners of starvation,
Arise ye wretched of the earth. . ."

The agitation mounted to a climax. In January and February, 1917, Petrograd seethed with unrest. Hungry workers went on strike in the machine shops and factories. Disaffection spread in the army; whole units deserted and men in uniform, some still carrying weapons, joined the workers milling about the streets.

Members of the Duma (Parliament) rose in that chamber to demand the Czar's abdication. Those in the Duma not taking such an extreme view called upon Nicholas to liberalize the government, to rid the army of incompetent generals, and provide some relief for the starving thousands by opening government food warehouses.

Czar Nicholas was living proof of the poet John Dryden's lines:

For those whom God to ruin has
design'd,
He fits for fate and first
destroys their mind. . .

With incredible stubbornness (or stupidity, as some believed), the Czar rejected every suggestion of his ministers to liberalize the government. He refused to relinquish any part of his power and when the members of the Duma continued speaking against him, Nicholas, on March 11, ordered that body dissolved.

The Duma disobeyed his ukase and remained in session. Mobs gathered in support of the Duma and suddenly rioting broke out in Petrograd. All the bitterness so long locked up in the masses burst out. There was fighting in the capital; great fires blazed in the streets as armed workers and mutinous soldiers battled supporters of the Czar. The rioting and insurrection spread to Moscow.

Garrison troops ordered to suppress the mobs turned on their officers and joined the demonstrators. The end was near for the despotic rule of the Czar.

On March 15, a delegation from the Duma's Executive Committee came to Nicholas, who was at

STARVATION!"

The Russian Revolution (1917)

Fierce-eyed Grigori Rasputin (far left), the bogus monk and holy man, is surrounded by high ranking men and women close to the Russian court.

At last in March, 1917, after weeks of riots and demonstrations (center, left), the Russian masses revolted against Czar Nicholas.

This photograph (left) of Czar Nicholas (center) surrounded by a bodyguard and members of the royal family was taken shortly before the Revolution.

The man of destiny in the Provisional Government was Alexander Kerensky (right). He became premier in July, 1917, on a program of keeping Russia in the war. Vladimir Ulyanov, alias Nikolai Lenin (far right), led left-wing opposition to Kerensky from exile in Switzerland. Non-commissioned officer (left), standing upright urges his men to move ahead during Kerensky 1917 offensive (below).

army headquarters in Pskov, and demanded his abdication. The Czar complied, saying "May God save Russia."

A provisional government was formed by liberal members of the Duma. The Czar and his family were placed under house arrest at the royal summer palace, and the new government went ahead with plans to continue the war against Germany. (Later, in 1918, Nicholas and his family were executed by communist revolutionaries.)

However, the provisional government had a rival for power. The left-wing socialists and communists formed Workers' and Soldiers' Councils (Soviets) in the army, the navy and throughout the country. The Soviets raised the slogan, "Peace, Bread and Land!" Guided by such men as Nikolai Lenin, who had been exiled from Russia for eleven years and was then in Switzerland, Joseph Stalin and Leon Trotsky, the Soviets agitated against the provisional government's war policies.

The government, led by Aleksandr Kerensky, ignored the Soviet demands for peace and instead, during July, launched an offensive in Galicia. For a brief time, the Kerensky Offensive made some gains, but the Russian army was riddled with opposing loyalties; Soviet agents had done their work well with German aid.

The Germans, sensing that Russia could be removed from the war if the Soviets took power, arranged to have Lenin sent into Russia from Switzerland by

Determined to keep Russia fighting the Germans, Kerensky brought troops from Siberia and, with General Brusilov commanding, ordered a large scale offensive against the enemy. Siberian soldiers in this photo are waiting word to advance.

A loyal Russian soldier menaces two deserters (below) with rifle butt in a vain effort to stem the tide of defection.

As the front was cracking up, the Communists staged an abortive attempt to seize power from Kerensky. A huge Petrograd demonstration was broken up by machine gun fire from government buildings. Note woman (center, foreground) shielding child.

providing him transport aboard a sealed railway car through Germany.

Lenin arrived in Petrograd to meet a tumultuous welcome; more and more revolutionaries gathered—Maxim Litvinov, Vyacheslav Molotov, Lev Kamenev, Grigory Zinoviev and others. These men spread peace propaganda among the soldiers at the front. Kerensky smeared them as German agents and urged his soldiers to keep fighting, but the average Russian soldier had no more taste for war.

The Russian army melted away; regiments, divisions, whole corps deserted and the Germans advanced toward Petrograd. At last, on November 7-8, the communists under Lenin rose in a bid for power. They seized the Duma in Petrograd and after a brief fight with a loyal women's unit (The Battalion of Death) and some officers, the Reds captured the Winter Palace and replaced Kerensky's liberal government.

The revolution spread throughout the land. Russia was in turmoil and chaos. Civil war raged and Lenin, seeking to save something from the oncoming Germans, sued for peace. An armistice was signed on December 15 and in March, 1918, after weeks of haggling, the Soviet delegation agreed to the peace treaty of Brest-Litovsk which stripped Russia of much territory. Leon Trotsky, the chief Soviet negotiator protested the harsh terms to the Germans only to be coldly answered, "Either sign or we shall destroy you!"

With Russia out of the war, the Germans—for the first time since 1914—had thousands of additional troops which could be used in the West. With the fall of Russia, the remnants of the Rumanian army also surrendered. No enemy any longer faced Germany in the East.

The Germans looked eagerly to the 1918 campaign and the chance to hurl their Eastern Front troops against the exhausted British and French. However, the United States had entered the deadly game with an unbeatable hand. . .

By November, 1917, Lenin and his followers were no longer to be denied. The Communists rose again and this time drove Kerensky from office. Backbone of Lenin's strength were dissident soldiers, sailors and workers (below).

Once he gained control, Lenin immediately opened negotiations for an armistice with Germany. He despatched his right-hand man, Leon Trotsky (below), to deal with the Germans.

93

"TO MAKE THE WORLD SAFE FOR

The U. S. A. Goes to War

Woodrow Wilson, 28th President of the United States, was re-elected for a second term on the slogan: "He Kept Us Out of War!" Wilson's margin of victory had been a slim one; he barely defeated his Republican opponent, Charles Evans Hughes.

The close election expressed the mood of the American people toward the grim conflict that had been raging in Europe for more than two years. Americans were not so sure that staying out of the war was morally right. Many had cast their vote against Wilson to show that they opposed America's passive role. Hughes had not favored war—on the contrary, he wanted the United States to remain neutral—but the voters used him as a protest against Wilson's pacifistic policies.

Back in 1914, not one American in 100,000 believed that the United States should become involved in the European fracas. However, the German invasion of

Belgium, the U-Boat campaign, the sinking of the *Lusitania* and unvarnished German arrogance, as epitomized by the Kaiser and the Prussian militarists, began turning American public opinion against Germany.

Although many Americans were of German descent, particularly in the mid-west, American sympathies swung preponderantly toward Great Britain and France, nations with which the United States had cultural and sentimental ties. Great Britain and the United States shared a common language and a common heritage; France was linked historically to America by bonds stretching back to Lafayette and French aid in the Revolutionary War.

But these emotional ties were overshadowed by the realities of the times. In their clumsy efforts to woo American partisanship, the Germans committed many propaganda blunders; instead of winning Americans

Woodrow Wilson, President of the United States, steered his country through two-and-one-half years of the European war without getting America involved. However, by April, 1917, Wilson was forced to state: "The extraordinary insults and aggressions of the Imperial German Government left us no . . .

choice but to take up arms . . . as a free people." Document shown is the joint resolution of Congress formally declaring a state of war between the United States and Germany. The resolution was introduced in Congress on April 2, 1917, and signed by President Wilson, April 6.

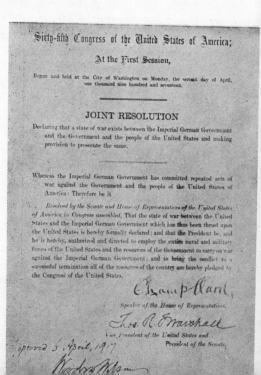

DEMOCRACY"

to their side, they created antagonism. On the other hand, the British were extremely skillful, as were the French. Stories of German "atrocities" in Belgium were amplified and spread; the German execution of the English nurse, Edith Cavell, was given wide coverage. Nor did the Germans aid their own cause by wholesale ship sinkings.

Also, German agents carried out acts of sabotage to cripple United States arms and munitions plants selling supplies to the Allies. The war goods were also available to the Germans, but since the Allies ruled the seas, the Kaiser could not haul the matériel; instead, the Germans resorted to the guerrilla tactics of arson and destruction. Among the worst acts carried out by German agents was an explosion at Black Tom Island, near Jersey City, New Jersey. Several persons were killed and many wounded in a blast that destroyed munitions valued at millions of dollars. The deed was

Columns of "Fighting 69th" kick up clouds of dust as regiment marches into raw surroundings of Camp Mills. Soldiers will be housed in tents (background) until barracks are built. Lumber for construction is piled up (rear, center) as workers and other civilians watch.

(Above) Secretary of War Newton D. Baker, tightly blindfolded, draws first number in draft of United States manpower which began June 5, 1917. Soldiers in New York's famous "Fighting 69th" lean out of Long Island Railroad car windows to bid sweethearts farewell as unit starts for Camp Mills.

ENLIST in the NAVY

TO ARMS
U.S. Navy Recruiting Station

PRO PATRIA!

JOIN ARMY FOR PERIOD OF WAR.

I WANT YOU FOR U.S. ARMY
NEAREST RECRUITING STATION

SPIRIT of 1917

"DEMOCRACY'S VANGUARD"

U.S. MARINE CORPS
JOIN THE UNITED STATES MARINES AND BE FIRST IN DEFENSE ON LAND OR SEA
APPLY AT POST OFFICE BUILDING LEWISTON, IDAHO

FIRST TO FIGHT

THE NAVY NEEDS YOU! DON'T READ AMERICAN HISTORY—MAKE IT!

U.S. NAVY RECRUITING STATION

Posters by James Montgomery Flagg, Milton Bancroft, and Walsh.

Army, Navy and Marines, all have their urgent appeals to the youth of the nation to bring their numbers up to war strength.

COLUMBIA CALLS

COLUMBIA CALLS

ENLIST NOW FOR U.S. ARMY
NEAREST RECRUITING STATION

Posters by Sidney H. Riesenberg, Shafer, J. Dougherty, Frances Adams Halsted (designer), V. Aderente (painter).

The posters reproduced here are a selection from the many which have been designed and made by artists to aid recruiting.

FOLLOW THE FLAG

ENLIST IN THE NAVY
U.S. NAVY RECRUITING STATION
HALL BUILDING, 161 GRISWOLD ST., DETROIT

traced to a network of subversive operatives led by the German naval attaché at Washington, D. C.

Americans were angered by this German sabotage, but the national temper blew up when the contents of a note from a German foreign office official named Arthur Zimmermann to the German minister in Mexico was revealed in February, 1917. Zimmermann proposed that, should the United States go to war against Germany, the Kaiser's government would guarantee to Mexico the return of its lost territories in Texas, New Mexico and Arizona if she waged war on the United States.

Combined with the renewal of unrestricted submarine warfare, the Zimmermann Note caused President Wilson to break diplomatic relations with Germany. When the U-Boat sinkings continued unabated, Wilson, after a soul-searching personal struggle, asked Congress in April for a declaration of war on Germany.

The man who had retained office because "he kept us out of war," now declared that the United States must wage war, "to make the world safe for democracy." The country responded with spirit and will. The nation that had been singing "I Didn't Raise My Boy To Be A Soldier," now changed its tune to "Johnny Get Your Gun!"

The small American army, about 100,000 regulars and another 100,000 guardsmen, was augmented

Finished rifles are placed in arms rack at Springfield Arsenal where workers complete more than one thousand weapons per day for fast growing U. S. Army. Bolt action 1903 Model Springfield Rifle was considered among best in the world.

Noted American artists such as James Montgomery Flagg, Frances Adams Halsted and others, gave time and talent to creating recruiting posters for the Army, Navy and Marine Corps (opposite page). Despite the draft, thousands of patriotic youths rushed to the colors without waiting for conscription.

Making soldiers of civilians was arduous work. Trainees (below) are seen going through rigorous bayonet drill at an army camp before being shipped overseas for advancing combat training.

by national conscription. The only other time Americans had been drafted into the armed forces was during the Civil War; conscription so went against the national spirit in 1863 that terrible riots against the draft had occurred.

It was different in '17; Americans went willingly into the service when the draft boards called. By June, 1917, Major General John J. "Black Jack" Pershing was in France with his staff. Soon, elements of the 1st U. S. Infantry Division plus a marine regiment came as the vanguard of the American Expeditionary Force (A.E.F.)

The Yanks were coming "Over There"; in late 1917, they arrived at the rate of 50,000 per month. On October 23, 1917, units of the 1st Division moved into the frontlines near Nancy; in November, the first three Americans were killed in action. And as the U. S. Doughboys made ready for the big adventure, the bluejackets and ships of the U. S. Navy were hard at work escorting ships, laying mines and hunting submarines.

Uncle Sam had rolled up his sleeves and was getting ready to make war on a large scale. Training camps mushroomed across the land, factories worked three shifts, and shipyards were busy around the clock. Everywhere one heard rapping hammers, clashing metal, and the cadenced tread of marching men.

America was at war!

Doughboys line up on dock carrying rifles and full field packs as they wait to board transport tied up at pier. Troops already on board hang on rail to watch new men tramping up the gangplank. Scenes such as this soon became common at every major American Atlantic port.

Four mounted officers of AEF are presented with bouquets as they pass through streets of Paris to plaudits of crowds gathering to see first Yanks in French capital.

With firm and forceful stride, General John J. "Black Jack" Pershing strides off the transport Invicta at Boulogne, France, on June 13, 1917. Pershing, commander-in-chief of the American Expeditionary Force (AEF), receives hearty welcome from French and British dignitaries. "Black Jack" and his staff preceded arrival of token American forces which formed the First U. S. Infantry Division.

ITALY'S BLACKEST HOUR

Caporetto (1917)

Italian troops hold trench in Isonzo sector prior to great Austrian offensive of October, 1917.

Even though the United States with all its young strength and boundless resources was now a belligerent, the Allies still faced dark days. Such a time came during October, 1917, when disaster nearly overwhelmed the Italians.

Italy had entered the war in May, 1915, anticipating a swift Allied victory which would bring vast territorial gains for King Victor Emmanuel's kingdom. But the Italians had miscalculated. Instead of a short war, they were involved in a long and costly one and Italy was unready for drawn out hostilities.

The Austrians, who had performed so badly in Russia and Serbia, fought well against the Italians. For two years, the lines on the Austro-Italian frontier see-sawed back and forth without decisive advantage to either side.

An Italian offensive in 1916 had managed to force the Isonzo River and capture Gorizia, but this victory was attained only after 1,000,000 casualties. Italy was growing war weary; her troops demoralized. All the blood letting and sacrifice had brought nothing but pain and sorrow. The dreams of a great, powerful Italy

Huge Italian mortar points muzzle skyward in sand-bagged mountain position. Guns such as this pounded Austrian with rain of high explosive shells during intensive mountain fighting between opposing armies.

Treacherous nature of warfare
in snow-covered Alps is dramatically
caught by front-line artist.
Austrian scouting party, right, is
swept to sudden death by
avalanche from mountain peak.
Horrified Italians entrenched at
left watch enemy's doom.

Difficulties faced by troops in
Italian Alps are depicted in this
drawing. Artillery pack mule is
being lowered by hoist from higher
mountain ledge to lower one.
Note signal man on left wig-wagging
instrucitons to comrades on
upper level.

Drawing romantically depicts
heroic stand of Italian rear guards
striving to check hordes of
Austrian and German troops pouring
down upon them. Actually, the
Italian Army did not halt the enemy
until November 7, when fresh
troops, reinforced by British, French
and American units stopped the
Austro-German advance at the Piave
River at the approaches to Venice.

dominating the Mediterranean and the Adriatic were fast fading. Instead came bitterness and disillusionment; by Autumn, 1917, the despair permeating the Italian Army had deep roots. Because they despised the commander-in-chief, General Raffaele Cadorna, many officers refused to obey his orders. All along the Isonzo Front, the discontent in the Italian army verged on mutiny.

Austrian deserters revealed that seven German divisions had arrived to bolster Emperor Carl's tottering forces for a counter-offensive to begin on October 24.

General Cadorna alerted all units to prepare for the attack, but no one heeded him. When the enemy, under German General Otto von Below, struck, the Italians cracked wide open at a place called Caporetto. An incredible rout took place. Regiments everywhere on the front left their positions *en masse* for the rear. Deserters ran eagerly to the enemy. Back and still back straggled the Italians. A stand was attempted at the Tagliamento River, but not enough troops could be rallied.

At last, on November 7, fresh, disciplined units were rushed to the Piave River at the approaches of Venice. The hordes of defeated soldiers pouring down from Caporetto finally halted there. At the Piave, the Italians fought furiously in defense of their homeland. The Austro-Germans were thrown back. The spirits of the Italian soldiers lifted when General Cadorna was replaced by popular General Armando Diaz and fiery Vittorio E. Orlando became the country's Premier.

Five British and six French divisions helped bolster the Piave front and all Italy thrilled when American units arrived to help stave off the enemy. Italy's blackest hour was over—the agony was ended. It had indeed been a desperate interval; Von Below's thrust had barely missed piercing the Italian heart.

On October 24, 1917, powerful Austro-German forces struck the war-weary Italians on the Isonzo front. At a place called Caporetto, the Italian lines suddenly broke and one of the war's greatest debacles took place. Italian troops are seen falling back in a disorderly mass (below).

(Below) *American Doughboys of the 332nd Infantry Regiment, 83rd Division, lob hand grenades into Austrian positions, somewhere on the Piave River Line, after the front had been stabilized, subsequent to the Caporetto disaster.*

DISTANT GUNS

The War in Africa,
Palestine and Mesopotamia (1914-1918)

From the beginning, the German colonies in Africa were doomed. A short-lived pro-German revolt in South Africa was quickly crushed; one by one the Kaiser's holdings on the Dark Continent were overrun. Only in parts of East Africa and Tanganyika did the Germans continue to resist. The brilliant German, General Paul von Lettow-Vorbeck, carried on gallant, but hopeless, guerrilla war in Africa against French, Belgian, British, South African and native forces, until November, 1918, when the war ended.

The campaign in Africa was a mere side-show compared to the struggle for supremacy in Palestine and Mesopotamia where the British and Turks fought bitterly. Stakes were high—the British-held Suez Canal and rich oil fields of Abadan.

From 1914-1916, the British and Turks fought in the desert; the going was slow and tedious without any material gains by the British who lost heavily in futile attempts to take Gaza. But in the fall of 1917, General Sir Edmund Allenby became commander of the British forces in Palestine. He was an incisive, hard-hitting officer, who captured Beersheba, drove the Turks out of Gaza and took Jerusalem, all between October 31 and December 9, 1917.

During his swift campaign, Allenby received invaluable assistance from a young British archaeologist, Thomas Edward Lawrence, who organized, incited and led a revolt of desert Arabs against the Turks. Lawrence and his Arab irregulars—mostly mounted on camels—raised havoc behind the Turkish lines; they cut communications, blew up ammunition dumps and raided outposts.

Lawrence, who would gain immortality several years later by writing *The Seven Pillars of Wisdom,* a

Native soldiers bearing the Union Jack pose with their camels and white officer during campaign in German East Africa.

Colorful and mysterious T. E. Lawrence, pictured in Arab garb, led revolt of desert tribesmen against Turks in Palestine. Known as "Lawrence of Arabia," the former Oxford student, archaeologist and writer, proved to be a master of desert warfare and was credited with a large part of British victory in Palestine and other desert regions. Map shows area of Lawrence's operations ranging from Beirut to Damascus and Jerusalem.

book about his desert experiences, captured the imagination of press and public. Lawrence of Arabia became a household hero. Yet, important as was the Arab revolt in beating the Turks, General Allenby, not Lawrence, conquered the foe.

Months before the Turkish Crescent was lowered from the ramparts of the Holy City, a dream fostered by both Bismarck and the Kaiser perished amid the welter of defeat in Mesopotamia. On March 11, 1917, British troops led by General Sir Stanley Maude captured Bagdad, the projected terminus of the Berlin-to-Bagdad railway. The vaunted *Drang nach Osten*—the Drive to the East—was derailed.

Bit by bit each German scheme for world domination was being checkmated on the global chess board of war. However, great struggles still lay ahead on the blood-soaked battlefields of France. . .

British troops take cover in ditch as hidden enemy troops ambush train on Uganda Railway.

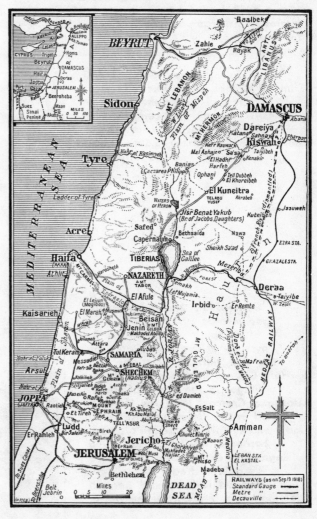

British tank rumbles over barren terrain of Gaza on Palestine border in April, 1917, as Tommies launch campaign to wrest Holy Land from Turks.

Strong-jawed General Sir Edmund Allenby (inset) who led forces that defeated the Turks in Palestine brought that campaign to successful conclusion for Allies, smashing enemy threat to Suez Canal and rich Mid-East oil fields.

General Sir Edmund Allenby and members of his staff enter Jerusalem on December 9, 1917, by way of the Jaffe Gate. For the first time in centuries, the Holy City of Christendom was no longer in the hands of Islam. Star and Crescent flag was lowered and British Union Jack raised to mark end of Turkish rule in Palestine. Earlier, British troops had taken Bagdad to end forever Bismarck's golden dream of Berlin-to-Bagdad railway and German domination in that part of the world.

"WITH OUR BACKS TO THE WALL!"

The German Offensive (1918)

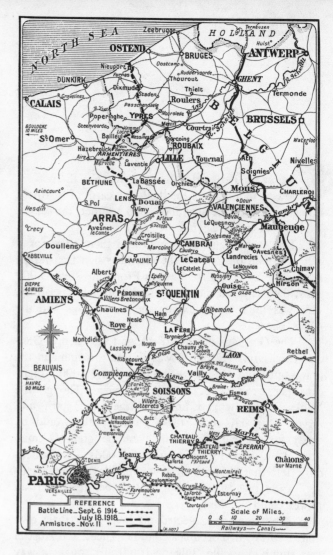

The Western Front showing the extent of the German advance in 1914, the inroads made by von Ludendorff in July, 1918, and the position of the battle line at the time of the Armistice on November 11, 1918. Note how close the Germans came to Paris in 1914.

Field artist sketches German trooper (above) with hand grenade poised for the throw. The two great German military leaders, Field Marshal Paul von Hindenburg and General Erich von Ludendorff as they appeared in early 1918 while planning the offensives of 1918 which were to have won the war for Germany before United States armed power could tip the scales for the Allies.

Spring came early in 1918. By March, there were wild flowers blooming in the shell-torn earth of Northern France, but with the arrival of good weather, the season of slaughter began again.

The British and French braced themselves for a great German onslaught. The Germans had transferred 1,000,000 men from the Eastern Front plus some 3,000 guns; they enjoyed numerical and material superiority. This was the time to exploit their advantage and the Allies knew it.

The Germans did not disappoint the enemy. General Erich von Ludendorff was chosen to command the grand offensive. He was well aware that 50,000 Americans per week were landing in France. Though the Yanks were raw and untrained they had spirit and fervor. One day soon, these green youths would be ready for combat; then, not even the great German army could hope to win against such odds. Von Ludendorff felt that a series of powerful blows now might yet crush the British and French before American power could tip the scales.

The Germans expected no help from their own allies: Turkey had been beaten to her knees, and Austria was stumbling while Bulgaria frantically sought a way out of the war. It was up to the Germans alone.

"As always we had to carry the burden for others," wrote a Berlin newspaperman. "We were paying the penalty for being the strongest, the bravest and the best!"

The German offensive opened March 21, along a 44-mile front on the Somme against positions held by the British. (Historians called it the Second Battle of the Somme.) Six thousand pieces of artillery pounded the British and the Germans broke through to register a 14-mile gain in four days—the greatest advance on the Western Front since 1914.

Just as Teutonic fury struck the British, the Germans opened a bombardment of Paris with a unique siege gun which had a range of 80 miles. The monster cannon was named "Big Bertha" after the wife of Alfred Krupp who manufactured it. "Big Bertha" created more panic than havoc with the shells she lobbed into the French capital; but, combined with the German success on the Somme Front, the appearance of the cannon sent Allied morale to its lowest point in years.

Even as the Allies struggled to slow the German advance, General (later Marshal) Ferdinand Foch was appointed head of all Allied armies in France and, for the first time since the war had begun, the Allies attained complete unity.

Von Ludendorff kept pushing toward the vital rail center of Amiens, but stubborn British resistance finally stopped him and the Second Battle of the Somme ended on April 5.

The Germans, however, paused only for a breathing spell. On April 9, von Ludendorff let loose his second thunderbolt. It struck south of Ypres on a 12-mile-wide front and was aimed at the Channel ports—Dunkirk, Boulogne and Calais. Known as the Battle of Lys, this German thrust started with an auspicious victory. A second-rate Portuguese division (one of two

Front-line photographer made this picture of German shock troops about to make a raid on enemy positions (above, left). Stock of hand grenades (middle) is ready for men as they hurry by on mission. Advancing through a wooded area with hand grenades at the ready, German assault party (above, right) heads for the enemy on the run. "Big Bertha" (right) hurled heavy calibre shells into Paris from a distance of more than 80 kilometers. Typical German shock trooper (bottom, left) laden with so-called "potato masher" grenades. Such men were specially trained to lead sorties against enemy trenches. Heavy German field artillery (below, left) was massed for monstrous barrages against British and French during von Ludendorff's desperate attacks of 1918. Artist captures violence of German artillery barrage landing on trench held by French troops (below). Fury of explosions knocks men from their feet. Note armored pillboxes and dugouts which mark this as a permanent position in French defensive system.

Although they lagged badly in tanks, the Germans built some big ones which went into action on the Western Front during von Ludendorff's big push of 1918. This unwieldy vehicle was captured by the French.

Germans employed a new and terrible weapon in 1918, the flamethrower, which shot out a stream of chemical fire. British troops are shown trying to repel a flamethrower-led attack.

combat units sent to France by Portugal) was astride the road the Germans took. The Portuguese were annihilated and General Haig had to rush up troops still resting from the Somme fighting.

By April 12, von Ludendorff was only miles from his initial objective, Hazebrouck, a great rail center. General Haig issued an order to his troops:

"... With our backs to the wall and believing in the justice of our cause each one must fight on to the end. .."

Good flying weather enabled the superb Royal Air Force to support their battered infantry by strafing and bombing the Germans, but von Ludendorff's men quickly captured Messines Ridge for which so many British soldiers had given their lives to capture.

Again Tommy Atkins proved up to the job of stopping the Germans; by April 29, the second phase of von Ludendorff's "End The War" drive was over. The Germans had made gains and driven wedges into the Allied lines, but they had not broken through.

The fighting had cost the British and French nearly 350,000 killed, wounded, missing and captured in about six weeks; the German losses were at least that high. The spring of 1918 would be remembered as one of history's bloodiest periods.

Von Hindenburg struts martially past saluting officers and men of crack Guards Regiment (above) just before opening of last-ditch German offensive in March, 1918.

Battle-scarred Canadian troops (top, right) are visited by Field Marshal Haig after they had made an epic stand during the Battle of Lys.

Von Ludendorff's thrusts were parried by the British and French, but only at great sacrifice. Wounded men lie on litters for removal to field hospitals at the height of the crushing German attacks which cost the Allies more than 300,000 casualties in six weeks' time.

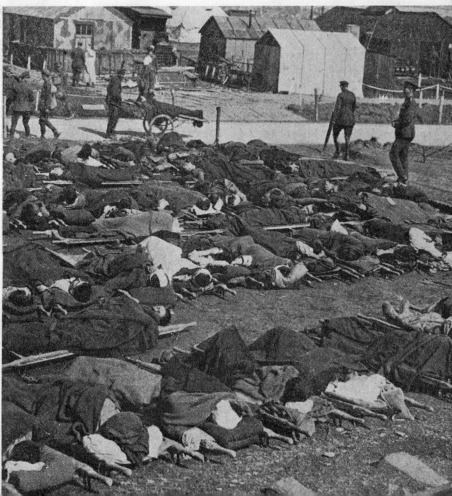

THE DOUGHBOYS AND THE LEATHERNECKS

Chateau Thierry and Belleau Wood (1918)

For a few weeks after the Battle of Lys, official communiqués reported "All quiet on the Western Front." Then, without warning, on May 27, that quiet was shattered as von Ludendorff unleashed yet another crushing blow.

This time his target was the French-held sector on the Aisne River. The Germans made the initial assault along a 25-mile-wide front which quickly took the dearly bought Chemin des Dames and spanned the Aisne, all within a single week.

By June 2, German advance units were again at the Marne having reached Château-Thierry about 50 miles from Paris. Marshal Foch looked about desperately for reserves; the only troops that had not yet been committed were the Americans. Everything depended on how the Yanks would behave in combat; although a million Americans were in France, few had completed advanced training.

But Foch needed men and he called upon "Black Jack" Pershing to supply them. Pershing responded with the 2nd and 3rd U. S. Infantry Divisions with Marine Brigades attached. The Doughboys and Leathernecks were rushed to the Marne in motor trucks and busses—the 1918 version of the 1914 "Taxicab Army" that had saved France at the same river.

The untested Yanks marched toward Château-Thierry; they could hear the guns now. Though these men of the 2nd and 3rd Divisions were not the first Americans to fight in World War I—five American divisions were already in the lines at various sectors— no troops had ever reached a battle area at a more crucial time.

As the 2nd Division's Marine Brigade entered Château-Thierry, French troops were pulling out.

"The *boches* are coming," cried a French officer, "you had better retreat!"

An anonymous Marine captain shouted, "Retreat, Hell! We just got here!"

The Yanks in Château-Thierry not only fought the Germans to a standstill, but also chased them back across the Marne. It was during the fighting there that the Marines were given a new nickname—"Devil Dogs" —by the enemy who said the American fought like "dogs of the devil."

At any rate, Doughboys and Marines helped the French stem the German tide. Near Château-Thierry, the Marines drove the entrenched foe out of Belleau Wood. If anyone had ever wondered how Americans could fight, he now had the answer.

While von Ludendorff's Offensive was reaching its peak, the U. S. 1st Division launched an attack against Cantigny, a German-held, fortified village. Jubilant Yank Military Police escort first enemy prisoners taken by victorious Doughboys, as other grinning Americans look on.

In June, 1918, the Germans reached Chateau Thierry and a hurry call for help went out to General Pershing. Men and guns of 12th Field Artillery are seen moving toward Chateau Thierry only 50 miles from Paris.

The Marines stopped the Germans but paid a stiff price in blood and suffering. A wounded Leatherneck is tenderly helped out of an ambulance at a clearing station behind the fighting lines.

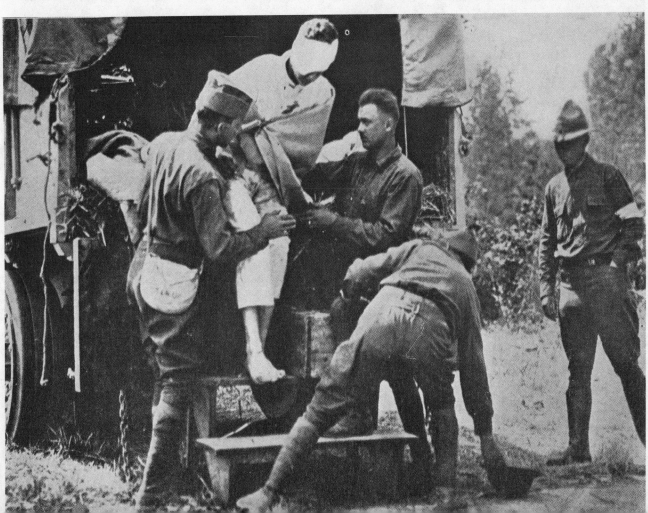

Hard-boiled U. S. Marines stand
guard at a barricade in Chateau Thierry,
ready to repel enemy counter thrust.

Throughout June, 1918, Doughboys
and Leathernecks fought Germans in the
thickets of Belleau Woods. A spirited
American bayonet attack finally drove out
the defenders. By June 26, the disputed
sector was firmly in United States hands.

Germans taken during the fighting
in Belleau Woods smile for photographer.
These young prisoners, mere boys,
show how badly pressed for manpower
the Germans had become after
four years of war.

ELEVENTH HOUR
ELEVENTH DAY
ELEVENTH MONTH

On July 15, in ninety-degree heat, von Ludendorff uncorked an offensive, known as the Second Battle of the Marne, to capture Rheims. As in 1914, the German hordes swept toward Rheims and Paris, but this time their blow had no chance of success. Once again, the Marne became a German tomb as Joffre's old war cry *"Ils ne passeront pas!"* rose above the roaring guns.

Von Ludendorff's attack ended in gory failure. Blasted by artillery, bombed and strafed from the air, driven with bayonet, grenade and rifle, the Germans fell away from the Marne with decimated regiments and shattered divisions. By July 18, the pendulum had swung from the German side. The Allies' turn had come to hit back.

That third week in July, Marshal Foch gave the order, *"En avant!"* (Forward), and the great armies he commanded surged forward in a series of overwhelming onslaughts that were not to stop until the Germans gave up on November 11, 1918.

In some sectors the Americans led the assault; in others, the British or French. On August 8, behind 400 tanks and a tremendous barrage the British struck east of Amiens. Years later von Ludendorff called this "the black day of the German army." A gaping hole

By mid-July, 1918, von Ludendorff's bid for victory had been smashed and the Allies prepared to strike back. Top-ranking officers of Allied armies planned strategy at historic meeting which included, left to right: General Henri Petain, Commander-in-Chief of French Armies; Field Marshal Sir Douglas Haig, C.I.C., of B.E.F.; Marshal Ferdinand Foch, C.I.C., Allied Armies and General John J. Pershing, C.I.C., A.E.F.

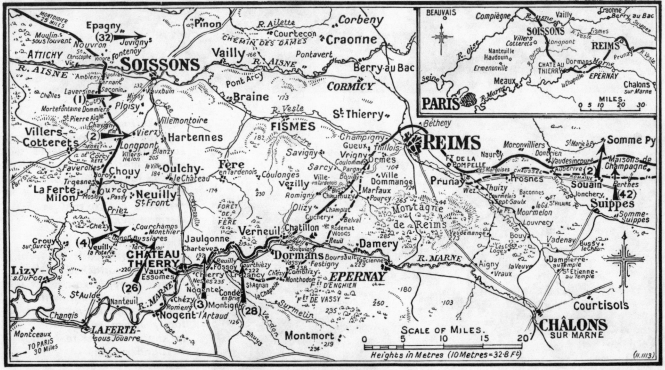

The British, French and Americans were each assigned specific sectors for the great Allied offensive that began July 18, 1918. Numbers indicate United States divisions during Foch's offensive.

Doughboys charging through levelled barbed wire in attack on enemy trenches. Man at the right has just been wounded.

was opened in the German lines, and the exultant Tommies raced through. Tank units roved the German rear. The British penetration was so deep that a trainload of reinforcements earmarked for von Ludendorff was captured en route to the front. An advancing tank detachment surprised a divisional staff at dinner and made the Germans their prisoners.

Allied pressure became unbearable and the Germans cracked. The Americans, fighting as a cohesive army, captured St. Mihiel. (Pershing had insisted that his men must go into battle flying the Stars and Stripes, under American command.) After this victory the Yanks streamed northward to Sedan, and at the end of September helped break the Hindenburg line by hard fighting. Throughout October, the Yanks fought a nightmare war in the Argonne Forest, overcoming furious German resistance.

Marshal Foch raised the cry, *"Tout le monde à la bataille!"* (Everybody to battle!), and the Allies lashed

U. S. Infantrymen (above) hug the ground waiting for supporting tank to silence enemy machine gun nest. Note second tank at right, almost hidden by smoke screen it is throwing out to confuse German gunners.

American machine gun section (left) heads for front. These men, attached to the French Army, have not yet seen action. Area through which they are advancing seems virtually unscathed by war in sharp contrast to battle-ravaged regions of Northern France.

Wearing gas masks, Doughboys in this startling photograph are storming enemy strongpoint. Yank on left failing to don mask in time is overcome by poison gas.

Foot-sore riflemen of famous U. S. Rainbow (42nd) Division (above) pause in woods for deserved rest after taking a number of enemy positions.

British Tommies (below) hold hastily dug support trench during brief lull in almost ceaseless fighting that raged throughout summer of 1918.

out on all fronts. Gallant King Albert's tiny Belgian Army came to grips with the hated *boches* and recaptured Ghent. The French, British and American armies kept slugging away with tanks, planes, artillery, mustard gas and swarms of eager infantry. The Germans tried desperately to stem the Allies, but disaster overtook them everywhere.

On September 15, the Bulgarians surrendered after offering a feeble defence against an Allied attack mounted from Salonika, Greece, by a motley force of Serbs, British, French and Italians under General Franchet d'Esperey.

Next to fall was the shattered Turkish Empire. The Sultan's forces in Palestine were routed. British planes annihilated an entire Turkish army, trapped in a narrow passage through the hills near Nablus. This was the first victory won by aircraft over ground troops. The defeated Turks begged for terms and signed an armistice on October 31.

The Germans now stood alone, except for impotent Austria, which surrendered November 3. The surrender followed revolutions in Hungary, Czechoslovakia and Yugoslavia, and a devastating Italian attack which routed the Austrians in Northern Italy.

Somewhere in Northern France, avenging French soldiers (above) storm German lines with grenade and pistol in an unbeatable assault.

These Doughboys (below), a patrol of the 166th Infantry, Rainbow Division, snipe at rear-guard German machine gun nest holding up the Yank advance.

Not even the iron-disciplined German army could withstand the unbearable pressure applied by the Allies during summer of 1918. Here (above), German troops holding a vital sector, flee in wild disorder, morale broken and fighting spirit destroyed. Hands raised in surrender, these Germans (below) are escorted to rear by rifle-toting Yank somewhere in France. Bedraggled German prisoners (bottom) stand in contented groups surrounded by American guards who herd them into shattered French village. Faces of captured men reveal relief that war is over for them.

Although the end was at hand the Kaiser stubbornly refused to yield. However, peace feelers went out October 4 when Prince Max of Baden, the German Chancellor, asked President Wilson for an Armistice based on the American leader's famous "Fourteen Points." (Wilson had earlier offered to the world the outline for a "just and equitable peace. . ." summed up in 14 main points that included "no secret treaties," "self-determination of minorities," and a "general association of nations to guarantee the independence of all. . .")

Wilson summarily referred Prince Max to Marshal Foch. "An armistice is the business of the military," the President declared.

The war dragged on, but not for long. The iron willed discipline of the German nation finally snapped; the first signs of the disintegration took place at the end of October. Sailors of the High Seas Fleet refused to obey orders for a final sortie against the British. Their refusal grew into mutiny; the mutiny became insurrection; the insurrection, revolution. Throughout Germany mobs rioted against the war and the Kaiser. Street fighting flared in Berlin and many other cities. Bavaria erupted into a full-scale revolution led by Russian-style

Defeated German Army (above) plods out of Brussels, Belgium, after having held that nation's capital since 1914. Sparse groups of civilians watch enemy withdrawal. As Germans march out, long-hidden Belgian flags are taken out and flown in defiance of the crest-fallen conquerors.

Not all Germans went to prisoner-of-war camps. This group (below) was killed defending trench mortar position against Doughboys of 16th Infantry, First Division, in futile attempt to block the way to the Soissons road.

Grinning Tommies are joyfully greeted by
citizens of Lille, France, as first British troops enter
that long-occupied city. Jubilant civilians
shower Tommies with flowers and cheers as happy
children eye the liberators in open adulation.

Soviets. The end could not long be delayed even though the German army still continued its senseless resistance. On November 9, Kaiser Wilhelm II abdicated his throne as armed revolutionary crowds carrying red flags tramped through Berlin. When garrison troops, called out to put down the mobs, joined them instead, even haughty Wilhelm knew his day was over.

Hours after the Kaiser's abdication Germany became a republic. A socialist, Friedrich Ebert, took over as president, and on November 10 the Kaiser fled across the Dutch frontier to live out his years in moody exile.

Meanwhile, representatives of the new German republic met with Marshal Foch and other Allied military leaders. A railroad car, drawn on a siding in the Forest of Compiègne, was the scene of the conference. At 5:00 A.M., November 11, an armistice which became effective at 11:00 A.M., was signed.

The welcome order "Cease Fire!" flashed along the thousand miles of war front. The guns gradually stopped and at the eleventh hour, eleventh day, eleventh month, a silence fell across the scarred battlefields. The war was over. The people of all lands rejoiced. For the 20,000,000 dead, the many millions of wounded, the numberless refugees, the war had ended too late. . .

A lone Yank guards the long, straggling column of German prisoners marching to the rear. For them the war is over.

Revolt in the Fatherland

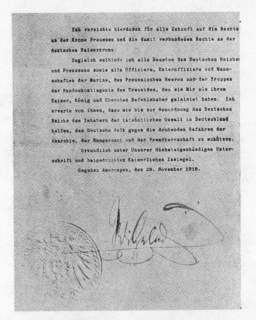

As German army in the field suffered setbacks, civilian populace grew restive. Hunger, disease and political dissidence spread throughout Germany. Troops guard butcher shop after food riot (above, left). Berlin leftists race through streets in disorderly demonstrations against regime of Kaiser Wilhelm (above, right). Popular discontent brings about abdication of Kaiser (right) and proclamation of German Republic (below) announced to gathering before Reichstag on November 10, 1918.

As defeat swept Germany, her Allies also went down in ruination. Bulgaria had surrendered at the end of September. The Turks gave up in October and the Austrians were decimated by the Italians. These ragged survivors of Austria's military debacle (left) retreat in despair.

All Germany's shattered dreams and ambitions are mirrored in the face of this woebegone German soldier (below). Only misery looms ahead for this crushed German who once arrogantly goose-stepped across Europe, beckoned on by visions of German world conquest.

Celebrations such as this one in New York
City erupted at news that Germany had signed an
Armistice on November 11, 1918, and
that the war was over.

Endless rows of crosses mark graves in German military cemetery.

Casualties of All Belligerents in World War I

Source: U. S. War Department

Country	Total Mobilized Forces Number	Killed and Died Number	Wounded Casualties Number	Prisoners and Missing Number	Total Casualties Number	Per cent
ALLIES						
Russia	12,000,000	1,700,000	4,950,000	2,500,000	9,150,000	76.3
France	8,410,000	1,357,800	4,266,000	537,000	6,160,800	73.3
British Commonwealth	8,904,467	908,371	2,090,212	191,652	3,190,235	35.8
Italy	5,615,000	650,000	947,000	600,000	2,197,000	39.1
United States	4,355,000	126,000	234,300	4,500	364,800	8.0
Japan	800,000	300	907	3	1,210	.2
Rumania	750,000	335,706	120,000	80,000	535,706	71.4
Serbia	707,343	45,000	133,148	152,958	331,106	46.8
Belgium	267,000	13,716	44,686	34,659	93,061	34.9
Greece	230,000	5,000	21,000	1,000	27,000	11.7
Portugal	100,000	7,222	13,751	12,318	33,291	33.3
Montenegro	50,000	3,000	10,000	7,000	20,000	40.0
Total	42,188,810	5,152,115	12,831,004	4,121,090	22,104,209	52.3
CENTRAL POWERS						
Germany	11,000,000	1,773,700	4,216,058	1,152,800	7,142,558	64.9
Austria-Hungary	7,800,000	1,200,000	3,620,000	2,200,000	7,020,000	90.0
Turkey	2,850,000	325,000	400,000	250,000	975,000	34.2
Bulgaria	1,200,000	87,500	152,390	27,029	266,919	22.2
Total	22,850,000	3,386,200	8,388,448	3,629,829	15,404,477	67.4
Grand total	65,038,810	8,538,315	21,219,452	7,750,919	37,508,686	57.9

Vizewachtm Johann Brommer
Kan: Gustav Harbach.
F.A.R. 53 • 9 Batterie
Hier ruht in Gott
Musk. Wilhelm Nitsche
2. Komp. I.R. 62
gefallen am 10.5.18.

THE PEACE THAT FAILED

The Big Four (above)—Lloyd George of England, Vittorio Orlando of Italy, George Clemenceau and President Wilson—presided over the long drawn out conference which brought about the Treaty of Versailles.

At the time of the armistice all Europe, almost all the world, boiled in chaotic ferment. The Allies rendered Germany powerless to continue fighting (theoretically, the enemy could have rejected Allied peace terms and gone on with the war). More than 5,000 cannon, 25,000 machine guns, 1,000 airplanes, tons of ammunition and other vital equipment were seized by the Allies.

In December, 1918, a peace conference convened in Paris. President Woodrow Wilson, who personally headed the United States delegation, was hailed by the masses as a savior, but his idealism brought no real peace to Europe. The great meeting formulated the Treaty of Versailles and sowed the seeds of hatred, frustration and future war.

The League of Nations, which Wilson had conceived, came into existence stillborn, for the United States of America refused to join that body despite the President's fervent support of the League.

Europe soon rumbled with unrest. Italy turned to Fascism under Benito Mussolini. The Nazi Party in Germany denounced the Treaty of Versailles and nurtured the myth that the German armies had not lost the war in the field, but had been "stabbed in the back" by Jews, Bolshevists and Socialists.

By the 1930's Adolf Hitler stridently called the Germans to fulfill "German destiny" and once more the thud of jackboots echoed throughout that land. Nazi Brownshirts marched toward a day in September, 1939, and the most atrocious and brutal conflict in all history. It was to end again with Germany prostrate amid the ruin, rubble and ashes of mad Teutonic ambitions...